DIY PR
Public Relations and Content Hacks for the Lean Start-up

By: Rebecca Hasulak

Dedicated, with endless love, to my Demi. You are my delight, my joy, my daily inspiration and my heart. I love you AFNMW.

Introduction

As the founder or leader of a start-up, you have your hands full. While already juggling myriad responsibilities, you've given some thought to the idea that your company might benefit from a public relations and content program. But, these fields are a mystery to you. You don't have the resources to hire a PR consultant (or full-fledged agency), and you certainly don't have the time to learn about – and execute – these initiatives on your own. You feel overwhelmed, confused and frustrated. What's a scrappy start-up to do? Give up on PR and content entirely?

Absolutely not!

DIY PR: Public Relations and Content Hacks for the Lean Start-up was written precisely for you. This book was designed to teach you the foundation of what you need to know about the often-murky world of public relations and give you actionable guidance on launching your own PR and content efforts. When you've finished reading, you'll walk away with an understanding of all the prongs of public relations and content, why they matter and an exact sequence of steps you can start following immediately.

Think of this book as a conversation between the two of us. I understand your challenges and am super stoked to start providing you with doable solutions. So, what are you waiting for? It's time to learn how to do your own PR, until you no longer have to do it yourself. Let's go!

MY PURPOSE IN WRITING THIS

Hi, and welcome! Before I dive into the subject matter of this book, I think it's important to tell you a little about why I wrote this and who I am.

There are a lot of things that this book is, and there are a lot of things it is not. I want to be upfront with you about my intentions with it as well as its limitations. This is meant to be a guide for you, the entrepreneur who has a need (or a want) to become savvy in public relations but does not know where to start. This is for the start-up that is still on the brink of glory and does not yet have the budget – or the need – to engage a full-service PR agency. This is for you, the business owner who wants to be empowered to understand PR and be able to use it to your advantage while simultaneously wearing the requisite 842 different hats that all entrepreneurs (and go-getters) must wear.

This book is NOT a replacement for legal advice (insert a "duh" here) and is not a replacement for strategic advice. If all goes well (and it should! I believe in you!), I most definitely recommend that you partner with a knowledgeable public relations firm (or solo PR pro) that can give you what I cannot: 1) customized strategies based on your specific company and 2) actual execution of those strategies. But, until necessity pushes you into that sort of engagement (and until your revenues justify it), consider me your new best bud and PR confidant!

Throughout this book, I'll shoot straight with you. My desire is to help you understand the basics of all things that fall under the large, often enigmatic "PR umbrella." I understand there are plentiful resources online and in-depth books about these exact subjects that I will be covering, but I don't really care because I'm not trying to replace or duplicate them. I am trying to do one thing and one thing only – give you a crash course in 'doing-it-yourself-PR' until you no longer need to do it yourself.

There may be areas I cover that you already know about (yay, you!), but I would still suggest reading every section because some parts build upon others. And who couldn't use a little refresher on their knowledge base? Sometimes you may read something you think is general knowledge and roll your eyes – but remember that this book is also meant for individuals who have had zero exposure to public relations. So yes, it is indeed educational and oftentimes basic. I am not trying to give you a PhD in PR because there is no need! If you want more complex answers to more in-depth situations, you can find those once you reach the stage of needing a PR agency. If we put this in terms of singing, I am not the voice coach who will get you to be Celine Dion or Andrea Bocelli. But, I *am* the voice coach who will prepare you to knock karaoke night – or that special song you're scheduled to sing at your sister's wedding – out of the park! When you're ready to headline your own show in Vegas, that's when you know it's time to call in the big dogs.

Lastly, as with any industry, many people have opinions about PR. What I am going to share with you is what I have learned through deep entrenchment in the field and actual experiences with clients. Sure, some pieces of advice are subjective. But, that's why I do PR and not something more concrete like math (FYI: numbers and I are not super cozy). And while we're talking about math, I want to remind you of something else this book is not... a marketing book. Marketing and advertising these days revolve largely around data analytics (ahem, numbers!) and software and highly nuanced strategies that are simply not my forte. I'm your girl for all things *PR* and *writing* related (nowhere does that say marketing). However, there may be a couple tidbits that tie into marketing mixed in throughout this book. Rest assured, I am in fact knowledgeable about those pieces of advice. But, those are the extent. If you want marketing, you'll need a marketing book (or agency).

This book is supposed to be fun and educational and applicable to your life and your business immediately. I've tried my best to make it interactive and accessible, so that you're not left wondering how on earth to translate something I've said into action.

I hope you have fun reading this, learning new skills and seeing some results after applying them! I'd love to hear your feedback and connect with you once you're done.

MY BACKGROUND

So, now that you know the "why" of this book, you may be wondering, "Why should I listen to YOU?" Good question! Well, in my humble opinion, there are a few reasons.

1. My bachelor's degree is in Communication, and – luckily for all of us – I have been told I communicate well via the written word.
2. I have worked on the editorial side of the public relations equation as well as the PR side of it.

3. I was an editorial assistant and later an associate fashion editor of a beauty and pop culture magazine, so learned the ins and outs of journalism and publishing.

4. I worked my way up from intern to a senior role at a highly successful public relations agency, whose clientele (mostly) included funded, B2B, high-growth companies. Many of these were in the technology field, and they ranged in maturity. The well-established, well-known brands gave me great training, but the start-ups I worked with while at this agency also offered me invaluable lessons (and were my favorite clients). I know PR intimately and understand how "modern PR" works, as well as how to use it as a powerful tool that can help your company's growth.

5. After my boyfriend and I welcomed our beautiful baby girl (17 months old at the time of this writing), I launched my own business, Quotable PR & Content. Through my company, I have worked with a wide range of clients, most of whom reflect similar stories to those of you reading this. It's a blast, but I can't work with everybody – and don't want any more hours because I am soaking up the time I have with my baby! Hence this book, which is my way of helping more people without having to increase my weekly workload.

6. I was raised in an entrepreneurial household! My dad has been a serial entrepreneur throughout my life and I have gotten the bug from him, by osmosis. He has seen the joys and challenges of working for oneself, and so have I. Our family has invested in him – and in his companies – and I understand firsthand the crunch of cash flow, the beauty of sales and the necessity of hope within small businesses. My boyfriend has also started successful entrepreneurial ventures, and I've been privy to these exciting journeys. If you feel misunderstood as an entrepreneur, I assure you that I will not misunderstand you. I know your time is limited, so I will try to pack as much information into as little reading material as I can. Most of all, I encourage you to hold onto hope! The life of a business owner is not easy, and it's certainly the road less traveled. But, high risks can equal high rewards (as the ubiquitous "they" like to say), so giddy up and stay in that saddle! Here we go!

Part I: **First Things First: Establishing the Basics**

Side note: Throughout this book I will refer to you as the "entrepreneur" or "business owner" or "founder," but in reality you might not be any of these things. Don't worry. As long as you are a leader within a small business or start-up who cares enough about your brand's public image to want to learn how to kick-start some PR efforts, you're in the right place.

Let's dive in.

MARKETING VS. PUBLIC RELATIONS

As I mentioned in the introduction, some aspects of this book will tie into marketing, but this is not a marketing book. To make sure we're all on the same page, I want to clarify what constitutes as marketing and what constitutes as PR. And again, some people may define these differently, but since this is my book, these are the definitions I'm going with!

Here are some truths:
- PR and marketing can (and should) work in tandem.
- PR and marketing should both also support sales, albeit in different ways. For example, PR should strengthen your brand's reputation, which will increase buyers' likelihood to buy from you. Marketing should make buyers aware of you and of your benefits, thus making selling easier for the salesperson.

Public Relations obviously has to do with your company's public image. Traditionally, *PR is everything public-facing that does not require a budget (or much of one)*. Based on these criteria, the following should be placed under the PR umbrella:
- Branding
  - Company Bios
  - Website Copy
  - Testimonials or Case Studies
- Content
  - Company Blog
  - Contributed Content
  - Profile Pieces
  - White Papers

- o   Press Releases
- Media and Analyst Relations
- Social Media
- Speaking Engagements
- Awards

Some may argue that social media qualifies as a marketing tool, or as an entity unto itself, but for our purposes we are including it under the almighty PR umbrella.

While all of these things have been "free" in days of old, the truth is that those lines are blurring a bit more now. I'll cover more of this later, but certain aspects of each of these categories can (and often do) require some money in modern times… but not always. So, we will still continue to keep them in our tidy PR home for the time being.

So, then, what counts as marketing? Well, as you may have guessed, marketing (or advertising) are typically those efforts that require a monetary investment. This can include:
- Direct mail initiatives
- Email marketing campaigns (the cost comes in when you use a marketing automation system)
- List or data purchases
- Ad buys (banner ads, Facebook ads, billboards, paid ads within magazines, Pay-Per-Click ads, et al.)
- Sponsorship at trade shows
- Search Engine Optimization
- Videos, PSAs, Commercials

This list can go on and on, but for now we'll leave it there. After all, this isn't a marketing book (tired of hearing that yet?).

Now that we've covered how we're going to define PR, you may be thinking, "Sweet! So, PR is free!" Au contraire. While you may not have to pay for each element of a successful PR strategy, a significant time investment is certainly required. And what costs more than your time? Probably not much. But, don't lose heart. I know your time is severely limited, so we will be going over ways to prioritize all of these facets to get the most bang for the time you have to commit.

IS PR IMPORTANT?

At some point, I'm sure you've asked this question. You may even have been asking it while reading this far (don't worry – I'm not offended). To be honest, I've even asked this question. There are plenty of people who will tell you that PR as we know it is obsolete... archaic, even. But, those people are wrong. With the endless advancement of technology that moves faster than we do, the field of PR is absolutely changing. We must adapt to modern times and acknowledge (and respond to) obstacles and opportunities that technology presents. But, I am glad to report that PR – as an ever-evolving institution – is still alive and well, thank-you-very-much.

So then, let's take a look at why it's important. If you remember two things about the "why" of investing in PR, they're this: credibility and awareness. Nearly everything we do in PR is done so that we either: 1) get public endorsements from people who aren't paid to endorse us, or 2) get more people to hear about our company and mission. Just think about it. Landing a contributed article in an industry publication communicates to your target buyer that you are an authority in your field. Winning an award tells your competitors that you're one to watch. Securing a speaking slot introduces you to a new audience and conveys to them that you have something worth saying. It's all about establishing yourself as a leading authority and helping your brand to gain traction through widespread awareness.

In a nutshell: Marketing is us paying through different mediums to tell others how great we are. PR is convincing *others* to tell the public how great we are. Can you imagine how influential that (typically third-party) validation can be?

Before you say it, yes... I know what you're thinking. Of course some aspects of PR don't fit neatly into this box, but the point is that most of them do. And the ones that don't (like blog posts on your own website or tweets on your own Twitter account) can still be used in conjunction with the rest. We'll get into that more later.

So, obviously PR is important, but is it truly essential? The honest answer is *sometimes*. At a certain point – and in certain situations – you need a good PR strategy to make it out alive. But, sometimes you don't. Sometimes you can get by without any (or at least most) of it. However, my fervent belief is that all companies can greatly benefit in the short-term *and* long-term by getting savvy and becoming intentional about PR and content right off the bat. And if you're reading this, you probably have an inkling that these efforts equate to time well spent. So, if that's the case, you might be ready for PR. Let's find out if that's true.

ARE YOU READY FOR PR?

If you're in the early phases of your company, you don't need a PR agency yet. Your company isn't ready for one, and you probably couldn't afford the expense anyway. But, you very well may be ready to start implementing some PR initiatives that can help your company scale.

Following are two versions of the same checklist to help you decide if this is the case.

For product-based companies:

- I have a product that is either patented or patent-pending.
- There is a clear, demonstrated need for my product in the marketplace.
- I have legally set up my company with the appropriate documentation for my state and type of business.
- I have sales.

For services-based companies:

- I offer services that I am qualified to offer (and have any necessary licenses that are required).
- There is a clear, demonstrated need for my services in the marketplace.
- I have legally set up my company with the appropriate documentation for my state and type of business.
- I have sales.

There are a couple caveats to these checklists. First of all, the "clear, demonstrated need" in the marketplace doesn't need to be super scientific. It can be as simple as, "my software program could be used in medical facilities." As long as you know there are medical facilities (which there obviously are) and no *exact duplicate* product already on the market, then there is a 'need.' Or, with a services company, you can determine this quite quickly. For example, if you deliver tax services, there is a need as long as people are paying taxes (which – spoiler alert – is probably forever).

Secondly, you don't need to have large volumes of sales to check the "I have sales" box. You simply need to have made a few sales or have a few paying customers. This is because sales, even in small numbers, validate the viability of your business. Furthermore, customers can be a priceless tool when it comes to PR efforts because we can use their stories, endorsements and praise in public-facing, helpful ways. We need permission for these things, of course, but we'll get to that further on. So yes, you must have at least a few customers and at least some sales to get started with PR. If you don't, focus on getting that right away and then pick this book up again as soon as you do.

Were you able to go through the appropriate checklist for your company and check every box? If so, congratulations! You're ready for some honest-to-goodness, homegrown PR.

A FEW THINGS TO KEEP IN MIND WHILE READING

- As you read through some of what is required to handle your own PR and content, you might get overwhelmed. Please don't get discouraged or start thinking it'd be easier to outsource everything or forget it all entirely. For starters, engaging with an agency requires a significant time investment. A functional relationship between a business and PR agency requires a lot of back-and-forth communication and demands on your time. Plus, it can really hurt you to overspend when cash is so tight in the beginning stages. This is when you need to be frugal and strategic with your funds. Trust me... for now it is actually much faster, cheaper and smarter to handle the prongs of PR that are pertinent to your business on your own – until you really have the time and resources to commit to properly engaging with an agency. Even if you can't follow all of my suggestions, you can take on *something* within PR that will bolster your business. It may not be everything, but small efforts can make a big ripple. So, please keep soldiering on.

- The best advice I can give you with PR is to start with a goal and use specific initiatives to work toward that. Keep your goal in mind with every phase of public relations and content that I take you through. Goal first, tactics second.

- Don't forget about the quality of your brand. PR and content are great tools that can help you achieve goals and present a precise public image. However, your biggest focus should be to have an ironclad business from the inside out. Treat your employees well, give precedence to excellent customer service, prioritize quality control and put processes in place to be sure that every individual who interacts with your company will come away with a positive experience. PR can strengthen you, absolutely. But, to have true clout among customers and throughout the larger business community, PR needs to be working on behalf of a strong business with solid underpinnings.

- You are a busy entrepreneur. You often don't have time to make a proper breakfast, let alone do everything I outline here. I get that. So, there is a reason for the sequence of sections in this book. I have roughly ordered each prong of PR to help you understand what should come first. Once you have mastered the first section – or at least have a decent handle on it – then you can move on to the next. If you think of it in terms of fitness, this is akin to getting in shape for a half-hour walk before you ever begin running. I do not recommend trying to start every part of every initiative at once because you will be vulnerable to slipshod work, too much stress, lack of quality and weakened results. Do one thing at a time and do it well. Then, when you are able to, continue on to the next thing.

- Here's one final note that piggybacks off of the last bullet point: While I do recommend proceeding in the order of the sections in this book, there are times when that may not make the most sense for your business. I'm not a mind reader and I'm not able to adapt this book to cater to every possible situation of every potential reader. However, there are a couple situations I mention below, which could benefit from an altered approach. Take a look, and if either of these scenarios sounds like your current circumstance, I invite you to consider the corresponding advice about what section you should start with...
  - Launching a product? Jump ahead to press releases and media relations.
  - Looking to attract funding or be acquired? Zoom straight through to case studies, customer testimonials and seeking third-party coverage. Oh, and consider starting to work with a PR professional sooner rather than later who can guide you through these tricky stages.

  If neither of these situations are what you're facing at this point in time, then I recommend starting with the first section and moving forward. In other words, you can begin with your web presence and cleaning that up. Then move to your blog, then to social media, then to customers and so forth.

BRANDING AND YOUR DIGITAL PRESENCE

Most entrepreneurs I've met love to talk about the pros and cons of their company "branding." Oftentimes, they will analyze and overanalyze the use of certain colors, fonts and images. Allow me to help you out here. These hang-ups are not only time-wasters, but they also detract from your goals. Yes, branding matters. But no, it's not worth the constant in-depth analyses, at least at this point.

If your company is in its earliest stages, you want to make sure you have the basics of branding covered – and then move on. Your company name, logo and articulation of your value proposition should all be decided upon ASAP. This isn't a book about branding, but here are a few elementary pieces to have in place:

- A business name
- A logo. The quality of your logo isn't something to shirk on. This will be stamped on your letterhead, brandished across the top of your emails and displayed on all your marketing collateral. There's an enormous difference between a professional logo and one that you whipped up using Paint. If you can, use a marketing agency for this. If you can't afford that, try to find a graphic design school in your area and see if you can commission a student (preferably a senior) to do it for you for much less money. Or, use a service like Upwork, Fiverr or 99 Designs to find someone who may able to do the job for you for less.
- Your stated value proposition. Avoid the temptation to make this cutesy. It should be simple, in real human language and quickly convey what you do. Stay away from language that is too colorful or descriptive because it puts you at risk of sounding cheesy or hyperbolic.

So, let's assume you have these nuts and bolts in place. Why does this matter with PR? Because every PR campaign or effort that you launch will hopefully pique the interests of potential buyers who will want to come visit your website! And your website is where these basics will live and shape most of your prospects' first impressions.

Your digital presence is incredibly important. If you can't spring for a web development company to mastermind a site, use a service like Wix, Squarespace or Strikingly to take advantage of modern, responsively designed templates that will help your site look clean and up-to-date. Okay, got that?

The next piece of the puzzle is your website copy. Chances are, you've gone through some sort of makeshift "messaging workshop" either alone or with members of your team. The goal, of course, is to pin down the words you want to use to convey your value proposition to prospects. This is another area that can be overanalyzed to the Nth degree. In an effort to save you time (and increase the value of your website), here are the five things you can do today to make your site more useful to your customer:

1. **Adopt a new persona.** You think I'm kidding, but I assure you I'm not. This will only be effective if you play along, so PLAY with me here! I know this isn't acting class and I don't expect you to be Morgan Freeman, but you have to pretend to BE your target customer for this exercise. Example: Are you a nutritionist who caters to men over 50? Great. Look in the mirror, and voila! The person you now see is Sammy Sampson, a 60-year-old man with diabetes and a deep desire to improve his health.

2. **Ask questions.** What questions would your made-up character ask? Write out the questions you'd want to have answered if you were in his shoes. Common questions are about cost, differences from competitors, credibility/expertise and how to contact you. Once you figure out what you'd want to know, write down your top five to ten questions.

3. **Browse your website for the "first" time.** If you're an involved business owner, you've seen your own website thousands of times and probably had an active role in creating it. But, for the moment, you are going to fall prey to temporary amnesia. You have never seen this website before. All you know is that you, Sammy Sampson, are seeking a nutritionist and seeing this company's website for the first time. Bust out that list of questions you created and objectively decide if your website answers those. Does it already? Super. No? Hang tight.

4. **Filter down to your top three messages.** You can stop being Sammy now. I give you permission! But, don't forget what you learned while in that role. Having approached your website with fresh eyes and a renewed outlook (one of a potential customer) should have helped you understand what will matter most to prospects. Let's keep going with our nutrition company example, so you understand what I'm getting at. Maybe for this demographic, the three key messages are: 1) Affordable, 2) Expertise in managing insulin in men over 50 and 3) An approach that focuses on simple tweaks for big changes. These messages are a combination of the company's philosophy, areas of concentration and pricing – and they're probably the three things that matter most to prospects.

5. **Cut your copy in half.** Once you have determined your top three messages, do one more website review. Your goal is to

reduce the number of words on every page by 50 percent. YES – that is half. I know, it's painful. And yep, I'm sure you feel very strongly that the one paragraph about your methodology is *so* important for people to see. But, the real, hard, cold truth is that no one is going to be reading that anyway because it's buried in an ocean of copy! If you're struggling with figuring out what should stay versus what can go, here are a few tips:

    a. **Align with messaging.** If there is verbiage that doesn't bubble up to your larger, most important messages (those three we established above), then cut it. For instance, our nutritionist entrepreneur might love the fact that he offers detoxing programs. That's great, but it doesn't reinforce his main messages. He can nix it from the site, and then find other ways to weave it into his communications (emails, newsletters, printed pieces of collateral, etc.). You can do the same with your less than necessary information. It shouldn't all be on your website, bogging it down.

    b. **Check your website stats.** If you have access to your website stats (which you should!), give them a look-see. You can check out what areas of your site are the most frequently clicked, which can give you insight into what prospective customers care about. It's not always a hard-and-fast rule, but generally the most clicked sections contain the most sought-out information.

    c. **Contact information and at least one well-placed call-to-action (CTA) must stay.** Never remove your contact information and never remove a useful CTA. Calls to action are more of a marketing thing, but these are triggers that invite your prospect to DO something. Keep them.

The final point I'd like to make about your website is regarding the layout. Just as you want your copy to be minimal, clean and chosen with care, your navigation tabs should be straightforward and make sense. Don't bury important pages with product specifics under a header like "About Us" because people won't know where to go. The more intuitive, the better. This may sound rudimentary, but you'd be amazed by how hard it can be to contact a salesperson or figure out what services a company offers just because of a poor website structure or a sea of unnecessary copy.

Part II: **Your Blog: Give Value to Gain Value**

Now we can move on to the fun stuff…. happy sigh (yes, I'm a raging geek about this stuff). Anyway, here we come to the blog. Some people may argue that a blog should not be housed under the PR umbrella. But, the fact is that many PR agencies now handle their clients' blogs, and many PR initiatives tie into (or draw from) a well-constructed blog. So, as far as I'm concerned, it's a valuable part of your public relations toolbox.

Being the busy entrepreneur that you are, you've probably thought to yourself that a blog is a nice cherry-on-top for brands who have it all together. Surely, there's no point in you spending precious time writing haphazard content that will be consumed FOR FREE.

Well, that's an understandable viewpoint to have… except for the fact that you're wrong (she says kindly). Here's why.

Yes, your time is precious. And yes, blogs are generally offered for free (as they should be). But no, your content should absolutely NOT be haphazard. And it is definitely not pointless or a nicety to consider only if you have everything else handled.

Blogs are like a support structure to everything else that we do. Think about public relations, and how almost all the content that you can hope people will read is generally produced through third party coverage. That stuff can be great, but you don't ultimately have a say in what gets said about you. A blog, conversely, is a wonderful opportunity to be in control of your message. It's also an awesome way to centralize important information in one spot. And it's a goldmine for giving your target audience a reason to come back to your website… again… and again… and again.

Here's an example. Let's say I'm mildly interested in writing a book (what a stretch!). I start Googling for information on how to go about doing this, and I find some great articles on a blog. I decide to start following this blog regularly because the insight into the world of writing books is so fantastic. Well, guess what? The owner of that blog is a publishing company. Who do you think I'd consider using for publishing purposes when it comes time to find a publisher? Exactly.

Your blog is also where you should give extra benefit to your existing customer base. In annoying corporate-speak, it's a "value-add" for whatever your customers have already purchased. And for the prospects who have not yet made a purchase, your blog is a handy dandy way to help them find you online (via search) as well as a way to give them value long before they ever write you a check. Helpful tips, industry updates and entertaining news should regularly be fed to your buyers (and potential buyers) through this avenue.

Still don't believe it's worth it? Here are some stats that should drive this concept home:

- B2B marketers that use blogs receive 67% more leads than those that do not (source: http://blog.hubspot.com/marketing/business-blogging-in-2015).
- Companies who blog receive 97% more links to their website (source: http://blog.hubspot.com/marketing/business-blogging-in-2015).
- Brands that create 15 blog posts per month average 1,200 new leads per month (source: http://kapost.com/content-marketing-facts/).
- Blogs are one of the most effective tools for increasing organic search traffic and are highly influential with buyers (source: http://www.business2community.com/content-marketing/34-compelling-content-marketing-stats-and-facts-01258894#VeTaWJmgYKaX2fmk.99).

That's just a small sampling of what's out there regarding the power of blogs for businesses. So, now that I've hopefully conveyed blogging's purpose and convinced you of its merit, let's discuss tactics.

I'm a big advocate of blogs for many reasons, but one is because of the opportunities they offer. For one, featuring guests on your blog can open doors to potential customers and scratch the backs of current ones.

Blogs are also fun because they're considered more of an outlet for opinions rather than a pinnacle of journalistic excellence. In other words, people are not likely to be fact-checking what you say or expecting you to be an award-winning writer! This is in no way an invitation or excuse to spew nonsense or get sloppy, but it does give you some freedom in the thoughts and advice you offer. After all, blogs are generally subjective and (most) people know that.

The ideal word count for a blog is somewhere in the ballpark of 400 words. This is because people want information, but they do not want to spend more than a few minutes reading. It's best to break up the content with either bullet points, sub headers or both. You don't need to do that if the content itself doesn't call for it, but it does make it easier on the eyes and more inviting to read.

Also (we'll talk about this when we cover contributed content), people are hungry for tactical tips in content. So, topics like "five mistakes to avoid" or "three things to do today" seem to get high response rates. This sort of accessible material can give readers a sense of hope and pending accomplishment. Also, curiosity is naturally piqued when someone sees a numbered list and doesn't know what those numbers correspond to. They want to find out.

Since blogs are more casual, you can have fun with them! Depending on how much flexibility you have with your chosen company voice, it could be good to get outside your comfort zone. This might mean a satirical post about something that's a common pet peeve of your customers – as long as it's not overly negative, scathing or offensive – or it could be a tongue-in-cheek approach that is playful while offering advice. It can also be a little self-deprecating at times, as long as you're not truly damaging the reputation of the brand. Everybody likes to have fun poked at someone else's expense, and if you can get a few laughs, it could be enough to bring your visitors back time and again. There's nothing wrong with levity in the right dose and circumstance.

While we're on the subject of negativity, it's important to note the Internet's proclivity toward it. People love to read things that they consider to be juicy or pieces that contain "insider information." While these posts aren't inherently terrible, they can take on (for lack of a better word) a yucky feel. There is a way to do this seamlessly and craft a post that interests readers without offending them, though. For instance, "the four mistakes all CEOs make," "what carnival clowns won't tell you," or "the dirty little secrets about champagne," are all headlines that would likely get responses and clicks, but don't need to bleed into defamatory territory. Write these with caution and make sure your overall message is still uplifting and informative.

Some companies will make the mistake of trying to use their blogs as a way to sell their services. This is not the time or place to do that. It will turn people off and lessen your chances of having loyal visitors if you are constantly plugging your products and being self-promotional. This is like the girl on Facebook who does nothing but brag about all of her work accomplishments. LinkedIn would be a better venue for her to promote her career skills and achievements, but on Facebook, she should be more personal and relatable. In your case, feel free to use other areas of your website to explain about your product or other forms of coverage to toot your own horn. But, your blog should provide value to your customers. I repeat: your blog should provide value to your customers. If a blog post naturally lends itself to a hyperlinked call-to-action or a product reference, that's okay. But, do so sparingly and only if it's an organic fit.

FREQUENCY

One of the main concerns I hear people express about launching a blog is that they don't have the time. It's the old perfectionist syndrome at play. Business Owner convinces himself that if he can't be churning out Pulitzer Prize-worthy blogs on a daily basis, he might as well not even start! After all, who would want to read anything less? Well, let me put the kibosh on that way of thinking. I have perfectionist tendencies like any other entrepreneur, but I'm here to give you approval to set those aside. Your blog does not have to be perfect; it just has to be interesting and informative.

The great thing about a blog is that you can change up the frequency based on your workload and other commitments. If you can only do one post per month, that's fine. More is better, but start with what you can manage and then slowly work up to more. As long as you aim to publish one post approximately every month (see all the leeway I gave you in that statement?), your blog will appear relevant and maintained.

If you consistently post less than this, then it's probably not quite time to get started. It's true that when visitors come to your site, they'll expect content to be recent. If it's not within the last month or so, they'll automatically (and not even consciously) start thinking you're dormant or don't care. But, don't let your perfectionist evil twin pop up to yell, "told you so!" in my face. The bottom line is it doesn't have to be perfect or grandiose or punctually posted at close intervals. It just has to be relevant, valuable and stimulating.

Oh, and many marketers will tell you that you have to put out large volumes of blog posts to make an impact. Sure, the most followed "thought leaders" are sharing blog posts daily. But they have different goals than you do, and one post a month will suit you just fine for now. Trust me. You can always, slowly and strategically, build up to more.

CONTENT CALENDAR

Remember how we discussed the fact that the subjects of your blog posts cannot be haphazard? Here, I'm going to lead you through the process of creating a "content calendar," which is every PR guru's best friend when it comes to managing a successful blog. It's another one of those basic ideas that actually works wonders when used properly.

The gist of this is that you will plan your content out about six months in advance at a time. You will do so strategically, and you will be able to prepare posts largely ahead of their projected publish dates (saving you time, frustration and panic).

A content calendar can be used and tweaked as you see fit. It's up to you to decide what works best in your case, but the sample I have provided in my digital kit (available for purchase at diy-publicrelations.com) is a good starting point. You can get fancier and include things like tags or customer personas you're targeting, but you don't need to.

As I mentioned previously, I recommend working six months out with your content calendar. Some people tend to get overly eager and think that planning further in advance must be better, but this isn't usually the case. The reason for this is that content mapped out too far ahead doesn't account for changes in your industry or business, or other situations which may need to be accounted for. You must be adaptable with your content. Six months out is generally as far ahead as you can look reasonably without having to adjust it all later. You don't want to spend all this time creating the content calendar just to completely redo things because something unexpected happened which throws off your planned cadence or content topics.

That ubiquitous "they" that we talk about say that variety is the spice of life. This is true, perhaps never more so than with content. Blogging is wonderful and generally pertains to text. But, you do not want to count out other types of content because you will miss out on engaging readers on other levels. Video usually elicits high responses and other fun things to include are infographics, pictures, or other formats of text (e.g. Q&A's, lists, etc.). When you plan out your content calendar, you'll want to designate if you are planning to use a different type of content for a certain subject. This will help you make sure that your content is varied and that you're never posting the same types of content back-to-back. For instance, you might do text, text, text, then video –then repeat. Or you might slot infographics somewhere in there. The bulk of your posts are going to be text, so make sure you intersperse other types of content every so often to keep it interesting.

The sample content calendar I referenced from my digital kit will help get you started, but here's the basic information such a spreadsheet should include:
- Topic
- If it's part of a blog series
- Expected publish date
- Type of content (video, infographic, etc.)
- Tie-in to other content (press releases, articles, etc.)

BLOG SERIES AND CONTENT IDEAS

Now onto blog series (plural). I always advocate for having a few blog series going on simultaneously, mostly because they're an easy way to think up recurring blog topics. Kind of shameless of me to say, but true. You don't have to be a content master to come up with these, either. You basically come up with a theme and then every couple months post a new piece that's part of that larger theme.

To give you some examples, let's say that your company is a landscaping company. Perhaps one of your series can be about seasonal subjects. This would mean that you come up with a cute and catchy name for the series and in every season you write a blog post that ties into that subject. For instance, in the summer your blog post could have to do with keeping the leaves out of your pool, so the kids can have fun over summer vacation. In the fall, it can be about preparing your lawn to be the setting for a haunted house for trick-or-treaters.

The same landscaping company could have a separate blog series, entitled "How to do _____ better." Maybe each month (or every other month), you post a step-by-step tutorial about how to do something with lawn care faster and with better results. It doesn't have to be rocket science; it just has to be something that's applicable for the people who might care.

A third series that this company might want to have ongoing is a customer spotlight. This one would include a brief snapshot of work done for a particular customer every four-to-six weeks. This would give other people an idea of what they can expect with this landscaping service and a look at real customers who have enjoyed the benefits of using it. It's also an easy way to create interesting content.

Another idea is to go big with whom you feature on your blog. Is there a company or person you would be thrilled to have as a client? Invite that person to take part in a Q&A for your blog. Sure, you might get turned down. But, maybe you'll get a yes, and maybe that initial interaction will lead to a future engagement. Even if it doesn't, you'll probably get a good piece of content out of it. Also, spend some time thinking about the individuals that your customer base would find interesting. Asking these minor celebrities/influencers/role models to be a part of your blog will show that you're very well connected, all while giving your prospects and customers valuable material to read. This kind of approach serves multiple purposes and solidifies you as a great resource.

Don't be limited, either, by only interviewing others for your blog or asking them to write guest posts you'll publish on your site. Get yourself out there too! You can open yourself up for some good exposure if you find businesses and other entities that are complementary to your area of expertise, and offer to write a guest post for them! Come up with a couple interesting topics to pitch them (and double check they don't already have posts published on the same subject matter), and ask to share your own thoughts with their readers. This can get some new eyes on you and your company, and also establish some goodwill with your peers.

A newer idea (that has, of course, coined itself a catchy term) is to "crowdsource" your content. This basically means to elicit the input of several individuals, and combine their thoughts into a single post. If you wanted to write an article about trends in naturopathic remedies, for example, you could consult four or five naturopathic doctors and ask them to answer a couple questions. Once you gather all the feedback, tie it all together into one cohesive article and be sure to draw attention to any themes you come across. And don't forget to give proper credit and attribution to the people who lent you their thoughts! This is a fun and relatively easy way to put together a meaningful post.

So, we've covered a variety of ideas for blog series or single posts, but perhaps my favorite type of content for your blog, out of everything, is that which centers on your client's most frequently asked questions. If you're not sure what these are, ask a sales person or customer service representative. The individuals who interface with prospects and customers every single day are sure to hear repeated questions and concerns. Once you gather a list of what these include, you can start creating content that addresses each one.

For instance, if you offer home goods that often require some assembly, you might want to write a blog post (or a series of blog posts) that give detailed assembly instructions for one of your most popular items about which you regularly receive assembly-related complaints. Another good idea is to talk about the most common mistakes you see customers make in caring for these items, and how to avoid doing the same. This will help your blog become a valuable resource to the people who buy from you, rather than just a collection of musings by a few talking heads.

GIVE VALUE WITHOUT GIVING EVERYTHING AWAY

I've heard many clients over the years express concern about blogging because they fear it gives away too much of their "insider information" for what they perceive to be too little gain. This is a common mindset in service businesses where the only way money is made is through the sharing of knowledge. This fear makes sense. Let's say you run a life coaching business where you help people organize their lives, maximize their time and improve their relationships. Your IP isn't a product and you won't get paid unless people decide to use your services and give you money in exchange for your time and wisdom.

The argument goes like this: why would someone need to pay you for your insight if they can just follow your blog and get all the same insight? If your articles center on the three main areas you tackle in your coaching sessions, then surely the need for your paid services will become obsolete and you'll have a thriving blog but zero revenue. It stands to reason to think this way, but this extrapolation is far from reality.

The truth is that if you start blogging, you can attract MORE customers. But, the key is to leave them always wanting a little more. I suggest you follow my three "rules to live by" when creating blog content:

1. Make it high quality.
2. Make it engaging.
3. Don't give everything away.

The first two are obvious enough, but the third one is what I want to focus on here. If you're the life coach we're discussing, pretend you have a trademarked (well, not officially, but in your mind it is) system for helping someone maximize the hours in each day. It's worked for others and you know it will work for future clients. So, how do you intrigue and inform prospects (and current customers), while still teasing your programs and getting clients to pay you? Here's a breakdown of my suggestions, using this example:

For your work on maximizing time, you have 10 key areas of focus you work on with clients. First, plan to only offer glimpses into seven of these via your blog. Then, within each post, only give limited amounts of the information that you typically would in a one-on-one session. End each post with something like, "Hope you enjoy getting started with these tips! To fully maximize your time, there are a few more secrets you'll want to learn. Try a coaching consultation with me – the first one is FREE – to get the full scoop!" You don't want to seem salesy in every single post, but this is a way to offer some of your "insider" knowledge while simultaneously stirring up interest in your services. You hook them with less than a third of your wisdom and reel them in by leaving no doubt they MUST know all your other tips (by becoming a paying customer).

IMAGES

We all know that people are visual creatures, and most of us can attest to the fact that visually appealing images within a piece of content draw us in more than text only would. Because of this, I highly recommend using one carefully chosen image to accompany each blog post you publish.

Stock photos – those that you can either get for free or purchase through royalty-free sites – are great in certain circumstances. But, since stock photos are used so much nowadays, they have lost their luster. While customers and prospects may not consciously think to themselves, "Oh that's a stock photo – how lame!" they very well may look at the photo and feel detached. They may even notice a lack of originality. The reason for this is that many stock photos look basic, staged or downright hokey. Let's say your blog post topic has to do with software. If you post an image of a perfectly ethnically diverse group of individuals smiling deliriously at a computer screen, you may come across as lazy and one-size-fits-all.

There are plenty of sites that offer royalty-free images that are more interesting and don't give off the stench of being a stock photo from miles away. Try looking for sites like Unsplash, StockSnap, and Stock-

Up. With sites that offer images that are a little more abstract and creative, you might not find the exact sort of picture you're imagining, but don't worry. As long as it is loosely related to your content, it should be better received than a standard stock photo. And don't forget that if your blog post has anything to do with numbers or percentages, consider including a pie chart or a graph or some other visual representation of what you're talking about. This is very helpful for people who learn better visually.

Part III: **Social Media: The Annoying Necessity**

I know, it may be a touch too harsh to call social media "annoying." But, can I call it a drag? Don't get me wrong... I have Facebook'd, Twitter'd, LinkedIn'd and Instagram'd with the best of them. In my social heyday, I even spent way too much precious time surveying my newsfeed and being enlightened about what my third cousin twice removed ate for lunch and the island my obnoxiously rich friend visited this week. But, can I be brutally honest with you right now? Social media is more of a scourge to me now than a source of enjoyment. Most of the time, I kind of even hate it.

But, you will notice that I tweet somewhat regularly and am semi-active on LinkedIn (or trying to be). As much as I think these "social" forums for being connected (between computer screens, through detached forms of interaction...) are pretty vapid and great at wasting people's time, they *have* become a staple in business. If you're a B2C company, your consumers will want to find you on the major networks. Yes, they'll sometimes complain to you this way. But, they'll also sometimes give you free, unintentional word-of-mouth marketing this way, which can be gold!

And if you're a B2B company, the businesses you engage with will expect to see that you're socially active and relevant. Even if someone doesn't intentionally seek out your business' social profiles to see if you're a living, breathing, modern company, it's a poor reflection of your brand if they do notice you don't have any (or stumble across a page that is dormant). It just makes you look antiquated at best and lazy at worst.

I'm by no means a social-media expert, and I don't want to be because I really am not fond of the whole thing (if you couldn't tell). But, I do want to give you a bit of guidance about doing the BARE MINIMUM with social media, so you don't damage your brand or detract from your other PR efforts. It's like in *Office Space*... Let's just get you those 15 pieces of flair needed to keep the job. (Anybody with me on this?)

Side note: If you really want to understand the nuances of each social media platform as they pertain to your business, I highly recommend the book, *Jab, Jab, Jab, Right Hook* by Gary Vaynerchuk. A good friend of mine works closely with Gary and played a big role in the development of the book, but that's not why I recommend it. It's an entertaining and informative read that will help you understand which platforms your business could benefit from most, what types of content to produce for each and includes real case studies of good and bad examples.

Anyway, onto our purposes. As I see it, a busy founder and his or her team don't have the time to maintain profiles on a bevy of social media networks. So, I recommend being moderately active on two until you have the manpower to successfully manage more. Here's how I would decide which two are most important for your company:

B2B → 1) LinkedIn, 2) Twitter
B2C → In one of the following industries: Food and Beverage, Hospitality, Services like Landscaping, Cleaning, etc. → 1) Yelp, 2) Facebook/Instagram
B2C → In an industry that is highly visual (e.g. Photography, Makeup Artistry, Talent Agency, Cake Maker) → 1) Facebook/Instagram, 2) Pinterest

This is very much my opinion and not based in any research. From what I've experienced, though, this is where companies can see the most results for their time spent on social media.

Now that we've touched on that, let me walk you through some tips I have for all of your social media pages:

- DO keep it consistent. In the interest of time and branding consistency, develop one "messaging document" that has long, medium and short versions of your company's story and value proposition. Extract from this central document verbiage of an appropriate length to put into your profile. Also, keep your logo and color schemes consistent whenever possible.
- DON'T forget contact info or a CTA. In the hustle-bustle, many start-ups' social media profiles leave visitors with no way to contact them or purchase from them. That's leaving money on the table, as "they" say! Make sure every social profile contains a link to your website, a phone number and email address. If it makes sense, also include a more formal call-to-action.

- DO use a scheduling platform. Some people say that these solutions remove the chance for interpersonal connections, but I tend to think the social part of social media is kind of a charade anyway. The fact is that you're busy – you can't be thinking up and posting one-off messages every day. Use a platform like Hootsuite and schedule tweets or posts a couple weeks in advance. You can still shoot off a random post when the urge strikes, but at least this way you'll know that you are being active without having to be beholden to sticking your face in a newsfeed every waking second.
- DON'T be an introvert, at least online. It's very important that you follow others who are relevant to your field (or just plain fun/fascinating), favorite or like posts that you find interesting and retweet/share others' posts if they're up your alley. And if someone bashes your company online, respond to them directly. Don't be defensive – empathize with them and do whatever necessary to make it better. Others will see this and judge you based on your response. On the flip side, if someone praises your company, thank them!! Give them some love and they'll adore you even more.
- DO keep it classy. I shouldn't even have to say this, but it seems like every week there's a "PR crisis" because of something someone said on social media. Don't be that guy (or girl). Keep it together and make sure every word you use and every image you post is in line with your company's values. If you're questioning whether to post something, just don't.
- DON'T overdo the sales. It's ok to occasionally tease or tout a product or service, but avoid being salesy or smarmy on the regular. This is a surefire way to get people to unfollow you and run from your company.

And finally, here is some advice on content creation:
- Holiday-related messages are low-hanging fruit. Queue these up in advance and you'll have at least one or two pre-set posts already taken care of each month.

- Other seasonal messages are always a good idea. If you have a seasonal product, find fun ways to remind people about it. Let's say you have a gingerbread cookie that sells only during December. Start teasing pictures of gingerbread or artfully snapped photos of the ingredients that go into them in the month or so leading up to the sale. You can get people hyped and prepare easy content this way.
- Provide value. Like with your blog, you want people to get value from following you. Offer industry insights or commentary on trending news.
- Pull short tidbits from your blog posts, and link back to the full posts.
- Comment on/link to other articles.
- Share quotes.
- Share fun facts.
- Share shortened pieces of customer testimonials.
- Announce time-restrained offerings or countdowns.

As a reminder, this is just to maximize your PR efforts through social media and to keep an active digital presence. If you want to capture leads or do anything fancy on social networks, check out Gary V's book I mentioned! I'm not your girl for any of that funny business. And now we can move on, thankfully…

Part IV: **Your Customers: Brand Advocates in Waiting**

When business owners think of their clientele, they often think of revenue or loyalty or relationships. But, one of the tools I've found to be least utilized (or improperly utilized) by start-ups is the all-powerful customer story. In this section, I'll guide you through the two main versions of a customer story you should be gathering and how to actually do so.

TESTIMONIALS

I like to think of a testimonial as the trailer of a movie. It should be relatively short, interesting and hit all the major points of the overall story. Testimonials are great for use on your website, in marketing materials and even in certain sales situations. The goal with a testimonial is to drive home the key benefits of your products or services through the relatable lens of a customer. These are written in the first-person perspective. Here's an example:

I absolutely loved working with Lightspeed Software! Every customer service rep I spoke with was considerate and knowledgeable, and the technology expert who offered me pro bono training couldn't have been more thorough. I will never fear new software again and will happily choose this company every time I need to implement a new solution.

CASE STUDIES

If a testimonial is like the trailer for a movie, then the case study is like the movie itself (although it actually would be more like a documentary). Case studies are in-depth and chronicle a customer journey from beginning to end, with as much detail and supporting information as possible. The goal with a case study is to demonstrate with facts and figures (a.k.a. "proof") how great your products or services are. These are written from the third-party perspective. Case studies can be used on your website, in marketing materials and in sales situations, too. Some publications even accept them to publish on their sites. In the section below, I'll outline more concretely what a case study should encompass.

ASKING FOR FAVORS

Once a business leader understands the different ways in which he can use customers to bolster the brand's reputation and strengthen PR and marketing initiatives, there often comes a big awakening. "Oh, so this means asking clients for the endorsements. Um, maybe I should pass." But, wait! I promise this part of the process is way easier than you're probably thinking it is.

First of all, most human beings are more than happy to help another human being when they have the opportunity to do so. And what are clients, other than human beings? I assure you, in the years I've spent gathering information for – and writing – endless testimonials and case studies, I might have had one person give me a "no, thank you" and maybe one other beg off due to a packed schedule, at most. So, believe me when I say that the odds are decent your customers will be willing to help you as long as they like you and your products or services. At this point, I feel compelled to insert a note: I implore you to never ask a customer for a testimonial or case study if they've expressed unhappiness toward you or your company at any point. This should be common sense, but I'm mentioning it so you don't accidentally damage an already suboptimal situation.

So, assuming you will be approaching customers who have been pleased with what you do, the next step is to do that – approach them. I've found the best way to do this is through email initially. You can choose whatever method you prefer, but most people feel like a phone call (or even worse, an in-person visit) from a vendor is a bit intrusive. This especially applies to members of my generation who look at an incoming call and automatically think, "Uh-oh, why do they need to reach me?" But, people of all ages who work in our modern world have adapted to email and often respond better to it.

Your email can be short and sweet, but should include enough information so the customer isn't wondering what they're getting themselves into. Here's an overview of what I like to send when all I want is a simple testimonial:

Hi Janey,

My name is Rebecca Hasulak and I work with Lightspeed Software. Austin Green gave me your name as someone who might be willing to tell me a little about your recent experiences with our company.

If you're willing, I'd love to set up a time for a quick call (10 minutes max!) and ask you a few questions about how it was to work with our team. Ultimately, we'd like to use what you share with me as a testimonial for our website and other marketing materials.

Let me know if you're game, and if so – when the best time is for me to call you?

Thanks for your consideration,
Rebecca

See how easy that is? You don't need to get into the super-fine details. Just cover the basics, ask for what you want and keep it friendly and light. If Janey agrees, make sure you bend over backward to accommodate her schedule since she's the one doing you a favor. And of course, if you know the client personally, just change the first sentence to say a quick "hi," and the second sentence to be something like, "I was hoping you might be willing to tell me about your recent experiences with our company." You get the gist.

Once you have Janey on the phone, ask her questions like:
- How'd you hear about us?
- Why'd you decide to give our products (or services) a try?
- What did you think of the ordering process?
- How did our services help you most?
- How was the quality of the final product?

Be sure to type up her answers as she speaks so you can reference exactly what she said. Now here is where it gets fun! Ready for a big reveal? A lot of well-meaning people think that quotes or testimonials have to be 100 percent verbatim. A dirty little secret of PR is that they don't (please contain your shock and horror)! You don't want to veer off drastically from the insight the client gave you, but you can have a little leeway in how you piece together what she said.

Start by reviewing her answers and recognizing any themes throughout that you can hone in on. You have permission (from me, at least) to restructure, massage and even rework the message she gives you to better fit your needs. I am absolutely *not* recommending deception, but I do recommend taking the core message she gives you and finessing it to align with your goals. And nine times out of ten, people won't even remember what they said on a phone call. It's unlikely you'll be called out for your slightly creative interpretation of their words, and even if you are, you can just be honest and let them know you were trying to polish up the statement a bit.

If, for some reason, the person does not agree to a phone call and answers your questions via email, don't take as many liberties with the final product. They'll know what they wrote (and can reference it), so your best bet is to stick with their words and just make minor changes for spelling, grammar and sentence flow.

Now, when it comes to asking for a case study, I like to go with an email that is a little more in-depth. Here's an example:

Hi Frederico,

My name is Rebecca Hasulak and I work with Lightspeed Software. Austin Green gave me your name as someone who might be willing to tell me a little about your recent experiences with our company.

I'm hoping to set up a time for a quick call (15-20 minutes max!) so I can ask you a few questions about how it was to work with our team. Ultimately, we'd like to use what you share with me as a case study. If you're willing to help us, the process would go like this: I'll ask you a few questions over a phone call, then write up the case study and send it to you for your review and feedback. Once we have a finalized version that you've approved, we'd like to use it on our website and other marketing materials.

Let me know if you're game, and if so – when the best time is for me to call you?

Thanks for your consideration,
Rebecca

As you can see, the overall message is still very much the same. But, the main difference here is that I spelled out the full process. This helps the client to understand exactly what they're agreeing to and how you intend to use what they give you. It also reassures them that they'll have ultimate control over the final version that gets used. This is important because customers often get a tad more nervous about the idea of case studies than they do with testimonials.

When thinking about a case study, you want to seek out customers whose stories with your company include some sort of hard data. This isn't always possible and it's okay in the early stages of your company to have a case study with general information, but it's always best if you *can* use concrete numbers.

Case study formats can vary a bit, but the overall structure is usually pretty standard. The goal is to present the challenge, the solution and the results of the customer engagement. Questions you will want to ask your client include things like:
- What were you using before you started using our products/services?
- Why did you start using our products/services?
- Did you look at other vendors? If so, why did you ultimately choose us?
- What challenges were you facing before you started working with us?
- What sort of solution did we offer to you?
- What was the experience like of engaging with us, from initial contact to where you sit as a repeat customer?
- What results have you seen since you began working with us?
- Are there any further insights or comments you'd like to share with me?

A few notes to keep in mind:
1. When you ask the customer to talk about competing vendors or their prior solutions, be sure you don't actually write anything vitriolic (even if they say it!). It'll just look bad for your company. Stick to facts and don't spend too much time

in the case study dwelling on why they didn't choose others; rather, focus on why they *did* choose you!

2. When you ask for results, try to get any quantifiable data you possibly can. This could be the number of days it took for a shipment to get to someone, the actual amount of cost savings a customer enjoyed thanks to you, a percentage increase in sales after a business brought you in as a sales consultant, the spike in website traffic a client had after buying your product (i.e. "3X as much traffic as before!"), etc.

Once you gather the information, it's time to transform it into a case study format. While you want the story to be compelling, case studies should be more on the serious, factual end of the spectrum and not as light as testimonials. Testimonials can get away with exuberance and exclamation points, but case studies should read more academically.

You can choose to use headers that actually say "challenge," "solution" and "results" if you'd like to, or you can weave interesting parts of the case study into the headers. For example, "challenge" could instead be "stuck in a rut with technology and sales," "solution" could be "upgraded systems and experienced new heights" and "results" could be "improvements since engaging with Lightspeed Software." There's no exact formula; just make sure you're conveying the proper information and giving as much detail as you can.

Even though the headings are self-explanatory, I want to give you a brief overview of what each section should include:

Challenge
This should explain what issues the customer was facing with her past vendor or solution. As mentioned above, don't be derogatory toward other companies. Use this space to explain why the challenge was causing the client grief, how it was impacting the company and why/how change was being sought out.

Solution
Rein in your urge to start this section with "TA-DA!" or "Voila!" or "Just in the nick of time, my company saved the day!" Reminder: case studies should not seem silly and are best without an excess of personality. Use this section to detail why the customer ended up

choosing your company and the specific ways in which your products or services solved the problems they were facing in the first part. You will ultimately paint the picture that you saved the day, but you'll do so by clearly demonstrating it with facts, which is much more powerful than just proclaiming your own biased opinion.

Results

This section is usually the shortest. You can either jump straight to a bulleted list, or give a brief blurb first about the types of results your client experienced thanks to you and then bullet out the specific benefits. If you have actual data, this is where it needs to go. Anything like "$5K in savings," "4X as many units sold," "10 weeks ahead of schedule" or "25 percent more qualified leads in half the time" will be perfect for this section. If you don't have actual numbers, just make your results sound as mind-blowing as possible without them. You can use phrases like, "more cost savings than ever before," "steady and surging sales growth," "vast improvements in keeping on-time schedules" and "significantly better qualified leads in substantially less time." The numbers are missing so these phrases are all weaker than the data-backed examples, but they still work and illustrate your point.

GETTING APPROVALS

So, you've written your testimonial or case study, based on information from your client. Now what? This step is honestly the most important of all. If you remember nothing else, remember that you must get your client's approval to share their words or story – and get it in writing. In business and life, I can sometimes be swayed into the school of asking for forgiveness rather than permission, but this is not one of those times. In this scenario, I belong to the school of cover-yourself. Do not run the risk of damaging customer relationships (possibly irreparably) or even facing legal ramifications. Even if a client agreed to a testimonial or case study initially, this person must actually sign off on the final product before you ever use it in any way.

Now that I've said my piece, I feel comfortable coming down from my soapbox. The good news is that getting permission on the final versions of your case study or testimonial is almost as easy as checking a box on your to-do list. All you need to do is email over the final version, with a message like this:

Hi Arthur,

Thanks again for taking the time to speak with me about your experiences with our company. I've attached the final version of the testimonial (or case study) we've pulled together based on our conversation, for your review.

Could you please take a look and let me know if it's approved as is or if you'd like to see any changes? We're looking forward to sharing your story once you give us the green light!

Thank you,
Rebecca

See how easy that was? If your client asks you to change some things, change them. Then ask for approval again. Once you get written permission to use the final version, you can feel free to use it on your website, in your email marketing campaigns, in your marketing collateral, in pitches to the press and however else you see fit. Good work!

Part V: **Meet your Ally and Constant Challenge: The Media**

GETTING FAMILIAR WITH THE PRESS

Before you even let a single thought about press coverage take up residence in your mind, it's imperative you take a minute to understand the people and processes on the other side of the equation. There are a few varieties and, while fundamentally similar, each represents a unique set of interests and nuances. It's to your advantage to not let these particular details pass you by.

Traditional Press

Traditional press includes any members of the media who have been around since long before the digital age. Granted, this is my own definition, but it's the easiest way I've found to describe this bucket. These people are typically conventional journalists. Many of them have gone to school to get their degrees in some sort of journalism, and at some point they've sworn to uphold the journalistic standard. They seek to gather objective facts and piece together stories that would hold up under the most intense scrutiny. They adhere religiously to AP style in their writing, and they would rather remove themselves from a story than taint it with their own biases. You can pretty easily identify this group. They are almost always the people with traditional titles like Editor (or any Editor-spinoff titles), Reporter, Journalist, etc. (or Anchor or Reporter if dealing with broadcast outlets). They usually are part of a well-established magazine, radio or TV station.

These people should be treated as true fact-gatherers. They want the essential information, without your skewed perception of it. If you have a product, they want to talk to customers to get proof of its marketplace viability. If you have services, they want numbers to back up the revenue growth you claim. They may seem cynical, but their skepticism is rooted in a desire to relay facts objectively to their readers. Within traditional press, there are a few different types of media that want different things:

Industry Press

Outlets that fall into this category are exactly as they sound; trade publications that serve your field. If you're in catering, for example, this would be magazines like *Food Network Magazine*, *Catersource*, *Cook's Illustrated* and so forth. These publications often want details since their audiences are so niche. Think about offering case studies, industry trend pieces (which are, as they sound, pieces centered on your expert opinion about a recent industry trend), product or company news and thought leadership (a.k.a. contributed articles). And as far as thought leadership is concerned, you're much more likely to land a contributed article in an industry publication than elsewhere, so I recommend these outlets as a good place to start with contributed content efforts.

Business Press

This subset of traditional press refers to the heavy hitters that most people in the business world would recognize by name: *Inc.*, *Fast Company*, *Wall Street Journal*, *VentureBeat*, etc. The competition is immensely crowded when it comes to securing coverage in these outlets, so their expectations for newsworthiness are understandably high. You're most likely to pique the interests of these journalists with news about funding, mergers, acquisitions and IPOs. In other words, they love money stories! Also, if you have any strong, data-rich business use cases, you might stir up some interest this way. In more recent years, these publications have also been accepting contributed content – but it's almost always from business leaders with pretty well padded resumes who have tactical, how-to type articles to submit (and catchy headlines). You could potentially get a contributed article in one of these outlets, but it'll take time and thorough research to understand how to deliver what they look for.

Broadcast Stations

When you're still in the early stages of your company, I don't recommend seeking out TV or radio coverage (although you may consider paying for ads in these places if your audience regularly consumes either type of news). Even so, it's still worth mentioning that these journalists will most often fall into the traditional press bucket. They adhere to journalistic standards and try to parlay objective stories. This is probably obvious, but TV stations like highly visual stories and radio stations like stories with captivating sound bites.

Non-Traditional Press

Bloggers

Now onto the more recent group of "journalists" that have come onto the scene – bloggers. As you know (since you are on your way to becoming one in your own right), bloggers don't need to go to school for journalism or even have the most impressive writing skills (although they should have the latter, in my opinion). In other words, all they need are 1) a desire to share their opinions, 2) a platform through which they can do this and 3) readers/followers. With the advent of social media, there are a lot of people who have acquired vast followings and whose words carry as much weight as those of traditional journalists.

Some people have a negative opinion of bloggers, but I'd caution you from adopting that view. Sure, bloggers are not held to a journalistic standard and can basically say whatever they want to, but they're not, by definition, bad people. They're just different from traditional press, and so they require different treatment from you.

Bloggers write similar stories to the other groups we've discussed, but they can be highly subjective if they want to be. If you're giving details to a blogger, just remember they are, more often than not, going to put their own slant on the piece. That could work in your favor, but it could also work against you. To get a feel for the type of story that could be written about you, look through the post archives of the particular blog you're pitching. You should be able to tell what sort of light business owners are often cast in, and whether the blogger seems to present facts in a fair way.

Another note: Some traditional magazines and newspapers now employ bloggers as an extension of their teams. Usually, their content will be housed under an "opinions" section, but even if it isn't, you should be able to tell pretty quickly whether their material is biased or unbiased. And, to make it even more messy, some members of the traditional press also blog! But, it's usually separate from their "day jobs" as journalists, so it's not too hard to weed out their mainstream pieces versus their blog posts. Bloggers are great to build relationships with, if you pursue those with quality followings and high-class writing.

Influencers

Bloggers were the new kids on the block for awhile, but an even newer group that business owners are now rightfully trying to reach are "influencers." An influencer is someone who typically has a day job within a business, usually in a senior role (but not always). These people have become figureheads for a certain industry – or topic – for some reason or another. Many times, they're seasoned speakers and/or have written a book. Almost always, they have built up an impressive social following.

These individuals are not usually writers by trade, but sometimes they do cross over into "blogger territory" if a publication asks them to become a frequent columnist. They do typically have a blog of their own, but what separates them from the bloggers we just covered is that they're deeply entrenched in whatever they're writing about. True "bloggers" write about things in their own sphere of expertise, sure, but blogging is also often their full-time job or a core component of their day job. Influencers, conversely, are living and working in their area of expertise. They lead in this area 90 percent of the time and may write or speak the other 10 percent. Because they're businesspeople and leaders first, their opinions tend to carry a lot of weight.

Influencers are different than bloggers and traditional press, too, because they're not often seeking a story. They write or speak as time permits because they want to or because they're passionate, not because they just cannot wait to tout news stories. These folks are a harder nut to crack than the other ones we've discussed. They might be interested in you, but it's best to focus on a relationship with them first rather than jumping straight into "please-publicly-endorse-my-company" territory.

The easiest and most effective way to do this is by following them. Follow them on social media profiles, retweet or share their posts, comment on their articles and try to engage them in a conversation. You may never get that one-on-one relationship you want, but you could! In the initial stages of business though, unless you have a personal foot in the door with one of these guys or gals through a friend, I don't recommend making them part of your PR approach right now. You may not make any headway, which can be demoralizing, and if it's all an exercise in chasing your tail, you've wasted considerable time. Once you've progressed in your business and PR efforts and are ready to engage with an agency, I'd fully recommend revisiting an influencer program and strategy with your PR team then.

Analysts

If you are in a field that involves advanced technology or a nuanced product, you should reach a point eventually where you regularly brief analysts. While this group is not technically press, I'm putting them here because they should be treated somewhat similarly. Analysts are usually members of a firm that employs really smart people to conduct research into industry trends and advancements, and then write meaty reports about them. These firms make a good portion of their money by selling such reports for astronomically high sums of money. Nonetheless, they are an important part of the business ecosystem and worth mentioning to you.

Since analysts are very intelligent, usually highly educated and extremely well versed in their chosen areas of specialty, they naturally have a lot of clout. They also are paid to be unbiased in their research, so endorsements by them are a huge stamp of approval that can be gold in furthering your business' credibility. They set the standard in predicting industry trends and keeping their fingers on the pulse of market news.

I wouldn't recommend approaching analysts during the youngest stages of your business, and here's why: these firms employ people who really know the ins and outs of their fields, probably even more so than you. Yes, you know your web development company better, but you could get on the phone with an analyst who wrote her PhD dissertation on agile development and literally wrote the book on the most cutting-edge development techniques being used today. This is intimidating, and could harm your brand if you are at all ill prepared and leave her with a poor impression of your knowledge (and company).

I would focus your time initially on true press and then ask an agency for guidance with analysts when you are at the point of engaging with one. The second way, aside from selling reports, that these firms make their money is when companies pay for their services. These contracts are usually quite costly and offer a way for you to get leading insight into your field straight from the arguably most informed experts. This sort of engagement can be a valuable tool, but you absolutely should be counseled on setting up and navigating such a relationship by a PR agency that has done so countless times. It's a huge investment to risk getting wrong.

When you finally do embark on an analyst program, you'll likely start with introductory briefings. These are similar to the briefings you might do with members of the press, but they're much more in-depth and get into the fine details of your technology or product. Expect to be asked the (very) hard questions and be met with skepticism and challenges. Analysts are great, but my experiences have been that they can be quite hard-hitting when interviewing founders.

Also, you'll be expected to have a slide deck (e.g. a PowerPoint or Keynote presentation) for a briefing like this and, if possible, a live demo of your product or technology. Most firms have a section on their websites where you can request an introductory briefing with an analyst, and this is the best way to try to land one (rather than emailing someone). Following the firms' protocol is important to them.

In case you're curious about looking into analyst firms, some of the biggest names are Gartner Research, Forrester Research and IDC. But, there are numerous others and some that cover very specialized areas of focus, so I urge you to speak with someone who can guide you through selecting the ones that are right for you.

MEDIA TRAINING 101

So, now you know more about the types of press there are, and the fundamentals of what they look for, but how do you interact with them? That's what this section is all about. Let's nix the mystique about dealing with journalists and make it an easy and fun process for you. This section is one of my favorites because, if done well, business owners can cultivate really great relationships with members of the press. Founders and other business leaders have a leg up with the press that PR people don't: guilelessness.

While many journalists respect and appreciate those of us in PR, others have been rubbed the wrong way, burned, or irreparably annoyed by our species and have therefore determined they will not work with us. That type of journalist might see a PR rep as a leech, an ambulance chaser, or a grade-A PITA. I love the journalists who are able to look past this stereotyping and appreciate what the good ones among us try to do, though, which is feed them news and make their jobs easier. But, some simply don't like to deal with PR people.

In any event, you don't have that barrier as an entrepreneur. You have passion, chutzpah and an earnest desire to share what you're doing with the world. This mindset and approach is often much more attractive to a reporter than a fast-paced, coverage-hungry PR shark. HA! But, really. The problem is that if you don't know how to communicate properly with the press (and give them what they want), your doe-eyed visionary advantages will be overshadowed by mistakes and you'll ultimately be overlooked.

So, I will break this down into bite-sized categories. Here goes:

The Nature of a Journalist's Job (and a Corresponding Crash Course in Etiquette)

Times, they are a-changin'. In days of old, reporters used to work on one story at a time with one deadline looming on the horizon. They would use typewriters, and newspapers and magazines would be physically printed. They had to work quickly and felt pressure, but they had relatively long lead times and the ability to focus on one piece at a time.

Fast-forward to the present day, and a journalist's life is much harder. Print is largely obsolete (much to my chagrin) and everything is digital. Since stories can be published rapidly online, there are faster deadlines and a need for more and more content. Journalists have to write MORE, write FASTER and write to beef up the newspaper's (or magazine's) analytics. They are under an enormous amount of pressure and usually not well paid. I had one reporter tell me that she has three articles due to her editor every single day, rain or shine, holiday or no holiday. THREE articles a day. And that's not even considered an outrageous number among her peers in the industry.

In addition to this obscene workload, reporters are hassled endlessly. Email is a great invention for most of us, but the group that wields the mighty pen gets overloaded with emails (often receiving several hundred each day – or more). People asking, begging for and demanding coverage for themselves or their clients hound them relentlessly. Sounds pretty ugly, right? Let me tell you... most journalists I have met are good people who care about the craft of journalism and want to tell good stories. But, they get pushed and stretched so much from so many sides that sometimes, they snap. And in light of their work conditions, I'd say that's more than a little understandable, wouldn't you? So, if a journalist doesn't respond back to you ever, don't be offended. Or if one of them writes back a curt response to an email, don't take it personally. They're probably pretty darn stressed or swamped or both.

So, with this in mind, how do you communicate with journalists in a way that is constructive for both of you? Let's start with what not to do...

Avoid these Mistakes with the Media

Mistake #1: Carelessness
This is huge and can cause a reporter to blackball you and your company for life. Really, it happens. Oftentimes, carelessness is an honest mistake, made by a busy businessperson who was hasty and trying to do too many jobs at once. But, even if your intentions were great, the end result is the same – you've irritated, if not enraged, somebody who you really want on your side.

There are plenty of examples of carelessness I can cite, and yes – I've made all of these mistakes myself at some point or another (shameful, I know). But, after having multiple experiences of going through the pain of being called out and wanting to crawl into a hole, I learned to use special care whenever pitching the press.

Let's pretend you're a company that sells a whole product line of supplements, and you're debuting a new type of vitamin that you think health-conscious folks would like to know about. With this as our example, here's how these mistakes might manifest:

- You found a reporter who wrote a story once about the herbal supplement market. The problem is, you failed to notice that article was written over six months ago and it was the only one on the topic that reporter had ever covered. This means you will end up looking like you have mass-emailed a pitch and didn't take the time to figure out if this topic was even something this reporter would care about. Bad move.
- You remember there was an editor who managed a "new products" section of a magazine you like. You find his email and send off a pitch! The issue is that the editor has since changed beats (he now covers skincare for the magazine) and he will likely ignore your pitch since you haven't kept up with his areas of coverage.
- A friend knows the publisher at a magazine and offers to give you her email address, so you eagerly send off the pitch with your press release included. BUZZ – wrong. You should've paid closer attention to her title. A publisher is not the person to go to if you're hoping for editorial coverage. (In this case, though, you COULD send a note asking the publisher if she could kindly connect you with the right person for news. That is perfectly acceptable, will maximize the connection and will show you've done your homework.)
- You're about to be acquired and you want to get the word out to as many publications as you can. You write a template pitch and plan to personalize it with each journalist's name and magazine title as you go, so you leave a highlighted "XYZ MAGAZINE" in the body of the pitch. But – oops – you accidentally leave that in there when you send one of your emails! Or maybe you changed it to the name of one publication, but then send it to the next one too, forgetting the other publication's title was in the body. I assure you, I've gotten a snarky email or two from a reporter basically saying,

"if by XYZ MAGAZINE you meant MY magazine…." or "sounds lovely, if I actually wrote for Reader's Digest." Don't do that. A good rule of thumb is to only leave the name part of the initial greeting blank to be personalized later because leaving other places throughout is a surefire way to forget about them or include verbiage meant for other publications/recipients. This looks careless and is highly irritating to most people. No one wants to be on the receiving end of a mass, template-based email.

- In your race to send out some ideas for contributed content you're super excited about, you've written to "Kiersten" at Forbes. That would've been awesome, except that her name is actually spelled "Kristen." This is a fictitious reporter, but you get the idea. Seemingly little boo-boos like this, especially when they're errors on a name, can have a long-lasting impact. Dale Carnegie said the sweetest sound to any person is his or her own name, and I agree. If you mess up someone's name, you're essentially saying who they are doesn't matter to you and they weren't worth one extra minute of thoughtfulness. Be very careful about names and their proper spellings.

- A final note about names… Don't be overly formal *or* overly friendly with the press. Almost always, using a first name is the way to go. If for some reason you can't find a first name, you can then use Mr. or Ms. Last Name, but generally avoid doing this unless need be. It may seem more polite to be formal, but it comes across stilted and stodgy. You want to relate person-to-person, not student-to-teacher or subordinate-to-boss. Be conversational and use a first name. And just like with the point above, be careful about the spelling of the name and that you're not making changes to it yourself. If you see someone's name listed as Jeffrey McGee… address him as Jeffrey. He's not Jeff to you – at least not yet. Don't assume nicknames. When (if) a reporter writes back to you, pay attention to how he signs his email. If it says Jeff, then you can feel free to say "hi Jeff" in your next round of correspondence and moving forward. But, always follow a journalist's lead. If someone ever called me "Becky," I would not be pleased and would probably write back, "That's Rebecca to you!!!"

As you can imagine, this list can go on and on and on. The main takeaway for you is to do your due diligence. Find out a reporter's beat (the subject matter they cover) and look at their latest articles to be sure that what they *regularly* and *recently* have written about jives with what you're presenting to them. Double-check titles and the spelling of names too.

Mistake #2: Verbosity

Remember how we talked about the demands on a journalist's time? Every individual in the job I have spoken to always says the same thing: your pitches need to be short for me to read them. I know you want to give detailed descriptions about your company, products or services and news or ideas (and don't we all?), but there's no need for a dissertation on the coverage you want to get. In a little, I'll give you an outline to follow for a pitch. But, just remember the fewer words used to convey your message, the better.

Mistake #3: Ambiguity

This might sound like a counteraction to the prior point, but it's not. Being clear does not require more words. As we mentioned above, you need to know what your point is, and get to it – fast. If you write a rambling, incoherent note about a variety of subjects, you've wasted the journalist's time and your own. But, beyond this, you also need to have a clear objective. Are you asking for an interview? A profile piece? Consideration of contributed content? There should be no question in the journalist's mind as to why you reached out. Be as clear as you can be as quickly as possible. It's absolutely okay to ask for what you want as long as you do so directly, tactfully and with humility.

Mistake #4: Lack of Respect

If you have a phone or in-person interview with a reporter, be early. On time isn't good enough. Yes, your time is important and sacred, but theirs is incredibly stretched thin. Make them wait, even a minute, and you're going to start off on a very bad foot. Also, be true to your word. If you get a response from a reporter and they ask you for something (a headshot, a bio, more information, etc.), get it to them ASAP. You could miss a great opportunity if you drag your heels and you could be perceived as disrespectful if you take your sweet time getting around to their requests whenever it works for you.

Just remember to have common courtesy and be appreciative of their time and consideration. There is no law that any of these people must write about you, so if they do – you're lucky! Last point on this: some journalists prefer to be pitched in different ways. You might not know what their preferences are, but if they do specify preferences, please adhere for them. For instance, an editor's bio may say "please pitch me on Twitter." If so, tweet them your pitch. If they ask for emailed pitches, email. Phone calls, call them. Each of them has a reason for their work process and the better you can fit into their routines, the more likely they will pay attention to you. Most journalists I've encountered do prefer pitches and follow-up to be handled via email, though, so I always recommend it as a starting point if you're unsure of their preferences.

Mistake #5: Playing Politician
If you actually get a reporter on the phone, or have one sending you questions that you've been asked to respond to via email, this is not the time to become Mr. or Mrs. Up-For-Reelection. In an effort to stick to topics that are comfortable, many businesspeople will try to veer off course when asked something they either don't want to answer or aren't sure how to answer. The best rule of thumb? Answer the question asked. It's ok to be brief, but it's not ok to run around a circuitous conversational maze simply because you're nervous. If there's something truly sensitive that should not be discussed, just let the reporter know that you're not disclosing information about that yet (and please do not say "no comment"). But, if it's anything else, face it head on! If you answer all questions asked (that you're capable of answering and have permission to answer), you'll end up having a much more positive relationship.

Reporters hate the runaround like everyone else, and will be able to sniff out the fact that you took them down a road about why you passionately hate the food at most catered events when they asked you how much money you raised at your last charity event. If you're like most of us (myself included), you're much less clever than you think. Be a straight shooter and I promise you'll make it out alive. Better yet, if you nonchalantly and briefly answer a question on a topic you don't love discussing, the reporter will likely jot down a note and move right along. If you hem and haw or nervously giggle, you'll draw attention to the area. And reporters are a lot like detectives – they can tell when they might be onto something juicy and they will do everything in their power to get it out of you! Stay safe. Just answer the question and move along. Nothing to see here.

What do Reporters Care About?

If you couldn't tell by the preceding sections, journalism is a business. Journalists are tasked with the difficult goal of captivating their readers' attention, when average attention spans are at an all-time low. By and large, the media really cares about its readers. The people who click on their stories are the people who keep ad checks rolling in, thus keeping their salaries paid. If their readers are happy, they have a job and their bosses are pleased with them. If readership starts to spiral downward or articles are read in decreasing numbers, this is bad news for the publication. Bosses will be nervous and will demand more from their reporters, and reporters will desperately try to create stories that will sell papers again (to use an antiquated term).

Publications care about their numbers when it comes to readers and clicks because this is how they sell ads. With this in mind, they want the best material that will engage their readers and keep them coming back. They need snappy headlines and relevant, timely material. They want to be the first to break a compelling story. They want all the trendy "how-to" articles, complete with listed numbers (i.e. "Five things to do today to get an editor's attention!").

But, while this is all at the foundational level, no two journalists are created equally. The type of media they're connected with, the role that they're in and the industry (and/or demographic) they cater to will all influence what kinds of stories they want to tell. Just because one reporter eagerly gobbles up a case study you send doesn't mean that another reporter will show even the slightest interest in the same thing. Don't be discouraged. If you do your homework, you should be able to find the right person for what you want to share.

Navigating Interviews

Call me crazy (actually, please don't), but we're going to go a little out of order here. In a later section about pitching the press, I'll get into why you might want to set up an interview with a member of the press and how to go about doing that. But, for now I want to assume you have already scored yourself an interview and I will walk you through the particulars of how this should play out. I want to talk about this here because we're in the section about the media, and interviews are a one-on-one time to interact with said media. So, let's begin. In other words, you've secured an interview... Now what?

There are a few types of interviews that are most common, so let's first figure out which one is imminent for you:

Background Briefing
This type of meeting frequently occurs at tradeshows or conferences, but it can also happen elsewhere. There will be a group of press folks that attend industry or business events to find out the latest about what's going in these genres. If you will be speaking at a conference, it's a great idea to book as many face-to-face meetings with relevant journalists as you can. This is a rare opportunity to meet in person, and doing so can help build a real relationship (and cement you and your company in the minds of the press members you meet). If you're just attending or exhibiting at an event, it still could be worthwhile to set up these meetings, even if you don't have a speaking session to use for credibility and bait.

Outside of tradeshows and conferences, you can still use a background briefing to introduce a member of the press to your products and services. If you're pretty confident (based on your own research) that a certain journalist would be keen to learn about your company, you can ask him to accept a background briefing with you. The same sort of conversation would take place as in the event scenarios, but the main outcome you'd be seeking is a "profile piece" (which is an article the journalist would write about your company). This is a great piece of coverage to land because it's essentially free advertising and third-party validation all-in-one.

The great thing about background briefings is that the press doesn't usually expect to be let in on juicy news. The idea is to sit down and lead the journalist through your company's history and story. You'll want to prepare a presentation (an actual deck) in advance, but don't be surprised if the reporter would rather just have a conversation. Be ready to proceed with the interview either way. Also, be prepared to lead the show. In fact, using the word "interview" to describe this meeting may be a little misleading because the onus is on you to keep things progressing in a background briefing. The journalist may ask you some questions, but she also may just take notes while you go through your whole presentation. This is normal; please don't overanalyze it or interpret it as a lack of interest.

Within this interview, you'll want to take the reporter through why your company was started, how you started it, what need(s) it fulfills, how you're funding it (although specifics regarding amounts do not have to be shared – and generally probably shouldn't be unless you have a significant round of funding to speak about), your customers, your leadership team and your future vision. If the reporter does follow up with any questions, she could ask who your competitors are, specifics on finances or for you to list out your differentiators. It's always okay to name competitors as long as you don't bash them. But, I'd refrain from divulging too much about your company's financial health. Instead, speak in terms of the larger picture or use percentages if you want to share something less sensitive than your complete P&L.

If you will be attending some sort of event, feel free to email the coordinator (or your point of contact) to ask for a media list. Be nonchalant, and be sure to mention if you're also exhibiting or speaking. You can sometimes get your hands on the full list of media who intend to attend. If you do, research each person to make sure they'd care about your company and then get busy personalizing emails that ask for one-on-one meetings.

Story Interview
This type of interview takes place when you've pitched a reporter a story idea (either about your company or about an industry trend) and he agrees to talk with you further about it. If you've landed an interview, the odds are good the reporter will actually write the story, but it's not a done deal until it's in print. In other words, you want this interview to be just as compelling as your pitch was. In this sort of scenario, you don't need to prepare a presentation. Just have some notes with you that you can reference while you talk. If you've pitched the idea of a profile piece on your company, be sure you have

all company messaging in front of you so you sound competent and knowledgeable.

In this case, the journalist will want to try to get a better idea of why your company should get its own story (a.k.a. free advertising). Before the call (or in-person meeting), spend some time thinking about what the biggest draw of your company would be to the journalist's readers. If the reporter covers new technology, maybe you'll focus on how your brand has innovated in a formerly stale industry to the benefit of the consumer. If the reporter writes for a parenting magazine, maybe you'll zero in on how your services save families time. Get the idea? Yes, your company is great in and of itself, but there should be a reason (or two) that it deserves editorial love in a grander context. Know what that is, and be prepared to articulate it during this conversation.

If you didn't pitch a profile piece, but rather an idea for an article about an industry trend, the interview will go a bit differently. You'll want to prepare your notes about the trend you're discussing, and try to have some data points available to back it up. Side note: be sure your data points are all recent. Sometimes people will find articles online and not realize they were published two or more years ago, which just looks bad. Double-check that any articles you reference were published within the last six months (or a year maximum). Then, be prepared to explain to the reporter why you thought this story would appeal to his readers and the specific commentary you can provide about the trend as an expert.

Resource Interview
A resource interview is similar to the last situation we discussed (about an industry trend piece), except that there isn't a specific story that's imminent. This conversation might come about in one of two ways: 1) You pitched an industry trend idea, and the reporter wrote back that she's interested, but that there isn't room right now for such an article – although she'd like to hear more about you/your company, 2) You pitched yourself (or one of your team members) as an expert in your field that the reporter could call anytime she needs an insider's take on your industry.

This type of interview is often the most laid-back of the ones I've described here. The main point of the conversation is for you to convey to the reporter why you have expertise in your proclaimed area, and to offer yourself as a resource whenever she may be able to use your perspective or a quote from you for a piece she's writing. It's still best to be prepared to talk about your company and its value proposition, but more than anything, you'll want to be ready to discuss your own achievements and authority in your chosen area since you're ultimately trying to win her over to using you as a resource.

A few guidelines to stick to when it comes to all meetings with the press:

- If you're using a deck, be sure that at least two other people have reviewed it for typos or other mistakes.
- If you're presenting on your own computer (either in-person or through using a screen sharing platform), close down ALL other windows – especially instant messaging programs like Skype or Gchat, email services like Outlook and anything else that could pop up on your screen while a reporter's eyes are glued to it.
- If you're meeting in-person, silence your cell phone and keep it out of sight.
- Before you begin the interview, ask the reporter how much time he has carved out for the meeting. Be sure to stick to his time frame, no matter what.
- Be early.
- If you're meeting virtually, log in well ahead of time and be sure to test all parts of the system (audio, video and screen sharing) so there are no kinks once the reporter joins.
- Remember all the other media etiquette tips I supplied you with, and apply them here too!
- If you're meeting in person, you have a unique opportunity to showcase your personality and passion. Make eye contact, be kind and take advantage of this setting to establish a real relationship.
- If a reporter wants an interview, but doesn't agree to meeting in-person or via a phone call, and prefers emailing you the questions to have answered in writing, that's okay too. This

option doesn't give you much chance to work on the human side of cultivating a relationship, but it does give you precise control over your message. That's one upside.

And just when you thought we were done discussing interviews, I have a couple final points to mention to you (you're welcome!). If you were working with a PR agency, your team would (or *should* at least!) prepare you by providing an "interview brief" in advance of your press meeting. This document usually includes information about the reporter, the publication, the purpose of the meeting, the reporter's most recent articles and some potential questions you may be asked. Since you're going solo, you won't have the benefit of having such a document handed to you.

But, I have good news. You can easily achieve this same level of preparation yourself. Just pull together all the details I reference above, and thoroughly review it all. A bonus of researching all this on your own is that the process of searching for each piece will make you even more prepared than if you were to read a document someone else sent you. Also, don't forget to think long and hard about potential questions. Even though you have no way to predict every question you might be faced with, you'll probably guess at least a few of them correctly. This will help you get a handle on the answers ahead of time. And I'll give you extra credit (worth at least three mythical gold stars!) if you also practice answering aloud extemporaneously. This is especially important if you're not used to speaking in a public forum. I'm well aware it sounds silly, but it will refine your skills and get you in the habit of delivering eloquent, complete answers – I promise!

Final note: If you're going to be speaking live, do not pre-write answers to use as a script! No matter how slick you think you are or how smooth you believe you can be at sounding natural, you'll come across like a canned recording. Total amateur move. It's perfectly ok to jot down bullet points or phrases you want to remember (if you think you might mess something up that's important!). And it's fine to keep your company messaging handy for reference in case you freeze up, too. But, please, I beg you, do not read answers from paper! Journalists will be annoyed at worst, amused at best. But, either way, your own uncertainty about your business will surely cause them to question your business' credibility - and your own.

What in the World is an Embargo?

The concept of an embargo applies specifically to press releases and breaking news, but I'm going to include it here because it even more so applies to conversations with the press. I like to think of embargoes as a sibling to an NDA that a company might ask you to sign before divulging trade secrets or inner workings. In the cases of PR, an embargo is essentially an agreement between you and the media that you will share some valuable information in exchange for the promise that it will be kept private until a certain date.

When you're in start-up mode, you probably won't need to mess with embargoes. But if you have an especially hot piece of news (like a major funding announcement or the addition of a highly noteworthy board member) that you are extremely sure media outlets will be clamoring to write about, they're worth considering.

The benefit to the media of this arrangement is that they receive the news in advance of the date it will publicly break, which gives them and their writers time to do research and write stories. It enables them to have really solid pieces ready to go when your news drops, instead of scrambling afterward to pull something together. The benefit to you with this arrangement is that it gives you a small level of certainty of coverage, which can be comforting. The fact that a publication agrees to an embargo reveals its interest in what you're about to tell them, and if a reporter invests time in writing the story, it's pretty likely it'll actually run.

But as with all things in PR, nothing's for sure until it's in print. Do not offer embargoed news of anything that is less than truly pioneering, influential or notable. Reporters will scoff at such an attempt, and you could end up embarrassed and/or seen as less than credible.

The other main thing to remember with embargoes is that they are not legally (or otherwise) binding. If a news leak could severely jeopardize the wellbeing of your company, skip the embargo offer and keep your lips sealed. There are many publications that will flat-out refuse to agree to an embargo, and some may even agree to one – then break it. I've had nothing but positive experiences with embargoes throughout my career, and always had journalists keep to their word. But crazy things do happen, and it's important you understand the potential ramifications of sharing news before you intend to make it public.

If you do decide to proceed with offering an embargo, you would first want to send a teaser email. It would state that you have some big news that will be breaking soon, and wanted to share it so long as they'll agree to embargo the information until a specific day, date and time. Be sure to specify the time zone, as well! Many reporters are on the East Coast and will eagerly push a story through in the wee hours of the morning wherever they are, unless told otherwise. If a reporter writes back to you and agrees to the embargo, then you can send over full details of the news. If you get no response or a refusal, then happily move along and keep your hot story to yourself and the media entities that care.

CHEAT SHEET: TOP TEN TIPS FOR INTERACTING WITH THE PRESS (aside from general etiquette, which I cover elsewhere):
1. Engage, don't sell. They want stories, not sales pitches.
2. Journalists eat, sleep and breathe deadlines. Ask what their time frame is upfront, then adhere to it.
3. Everyone wants a new story! Don't give the same one to several media outlets. You will be found out and you will have a hard time convincing one of these "duped" journalists to trust that you have a fresh story ever again.
4. *Nothing* is "off the record." Everything you say can – and probably will – end up in print, no matter how tight you think you are with a reporter. Don't be lured in by complacency-inducing phrases like "between you and me" or "just to satisfy my own curiosity" either... these mean the same thing and they still offer you zero guarantees.
5. Always be uplifting or neutral when talking about competitors. Trash talk will only come back to bite you.
6. Speak in concrete truths. Speculation makes you look ill prepared and can be perceived as lying if your claims can't be backed up. If you don't know something, be honest and say, "I

don't know" or "I'm not sure, but I'll find out and get back to you on that."

7. Once the message you give to reporters is out of your hands, they are in control. You can no longer dictate how it's ultimately relayed because it is now theirs to absorb and retell.

8. Never ask to see an article before it's published.

9. If you're unsure what a reporter is asking for or unclear about something, please ask. It's far better than making assumptions!

10. Be nice. Nice guys – and ladies – finish first with the media.

Part VI: **Public Relations: The Grunt Work behind the Glamour**

I can guess what you're thinking... "Rebecca, we're just getting to the PR part of this book now? What was all the rest of this about?" But, fear not. This entire book is in fact all about PR (what a big reveal). This section just happens to zoom in on some of the efforts most traditionally associated with the public relations field. So, go ahead... keep reading!

THE ALMIGHTY PRESS RELEASE

Note: For this section and the subsequent one about newswires, I wanted to bring you as much information as possible since, in my experience, press releases and newswires are two of the most misunderstood PR tools – even by many PR people. So, to beef up the perspective I could offer you, I turned to a colleague I've had the pleasure of working with over the years for some further information. An incredibly knowledgeable business leader, he spent a considerable amount of his career in a senior role at one of the most prestigious newswire companies. He's no longer in this role, but his insights are priceless. Throughout the next two sections, I've interspersed his ideas (noted with italics) amidst my own. I hope you enjoy learning from what he has to say!

Oh, press releases. While some argue that the press release is out-of-date, I have deduced through extensive experience speaking and working with numerous journalists over the years that it is not – at least not yet.

But, I'll shoot straight with you – press releases can be the bane of a PR person's existence. The reason isn't because the format is contrived (it is) or because the content can be dry (although that's often the case)... it's because clients do not understand them. I cannot tell you how many smart business owners have come to me (or an agency) and asked for a press release for some "news" that really wasn't. (Deep breaths, Rebecca, deep breaths.)

Before we continue on to how to use press releases properly, I must ask for your undivided attention for a minute. Let's chat about NEWS.

What news *is*: Something that impacts the consumer, business or group of media whose attention you want to get. This could include things like a new business launch, a new (or updated) product or service offering, funding, an acquisition, an IPO, new leadership/changed business structure, company growth (usually with one or more of the following to substantiate it: award wins, revenue growth, hiring, newly signed customers, new office space, etc.). It really is anything that truly fulfills the first sentence of this paragraph.

What news *is not*: Something that matters to your company, but probably few others. Anything strictly self-serving falls into this bucket, including (but certainly not limited to): someone from your company speaking at an event, your company putting on a webinar, your CEO attending a conference, an updated handbook your company compiled regarding HR policies, etc.

It might seem silly to get worked up about this, but it's frustrating to see savvy businesspeople shoot themselves in the foot and waste time on initiatives that do not serve them. It's a joke in the PR world that everything a client does is "newsworthy" or "breaking news" because most businesses think that's the case with every single move they make, while most news outlets would vehemently disagree. That probably makes PR folks sound jerky, but it's all in good fun. In truth, I understand where you're coming from! Everything your business does *is* huge to you. As a start-up, the little decisions and minor wins can mean a great deal to you. And they should. But, this doesn't mean that journalists (or consumers) will care about these things.

Please don't take it personally. Again, journalism is a business. If you were clicking through Yahoo! News or something similar, and saw a headline that read "Founder Jeremiah Jamison Attends CNET Conference," would you click it? Be honest. You would not.

You may be thinking, but wait – publications write about silly things like what shoes Amal Clooney is wearing or the fact that SnapChat's CEO is speaking at a podunk college. Yep. The world isn't fair. But, these people are famous, and so the continuum of what's newsworthy in their lives or businesses is unfairly skewed. It goes something like this: The more famous you are, the more the mundane aspects of your life count as "news." The less famous you are, the more high-impact aspects of your life must be to be covered at all.

It seems wrong, but it's, again, all about giving readers what they want. For whatever reason, our weird celebrity culture has made it so that fame is fascinating and stories tied to famous people drive clicks, which drive ad buys, which increase revenues, etc.... whereas moderately compelling news from Smith Start-up simply doesn't do anything for a publication. Unless, of course, you have true news that genuinely impacts consumers, businesses or media groups.

The positive part of this depressing diatribe is that our culture is evolving to care more about business and entrepreneurship. Publications like *Inc.* and *TechCrunch*, and TV shows like *The Profit* and *Shark Tank*, all cater to a society that is increasingly interested in becoming their own bosses and gaining freedom in their lives. Hopefully this focus will continue to trend, and we might see a shift in the types of stories that are most popular. But, for now, it's important to remember that you should have something very captivating to share if you're going to distribute it as a press release.

Beyond merely deciding to share news through the press release vehicle, there are additional options to consider. Using a newswire to send out the news is the most traditional approach. We'll get into newswires in-depth in the next section, but distributing a press release this way costs money.

If you have something important, but not necessarily newsworthy to write about, you can take more of a manual approach. You could write up a press release about it and then post it straight to your website. You'll save hundreds of dollars by not sending it out "over the wire," but still have all the pertinent information centralized in one place and in one official format. This is good for things like single award wins that aren't major enough to attract the eye of a journalist or announcements that won't impact your target audience, but may be important for your internal team's morale.

Then there are times that a full press release is overkill, like if you're hosting an event. Instead, a media alert would be a good option here. A media alert is like an abridged press release, that just includes the "who, what, when, where, why" components of the news. This is an easy way for journalists to get your information, but not be bogged down by unnecessary copy. You wouldn't typically want to dole out the expense of sending a media alert out over the wire, but instead could manually send it to individual journalists whose prior coverage leads you to believe they – and their readers – would care about such an event.

Another note about events: Most cities have multiple public calendars that people visit to find activities and things to do. These are often tied to public entities, publications' websites or associations' websites. You can usually submit your event for inclusion in such calendars for free, but sometimes you have to pay to be included. If you're trying to get publicity for an event, they're a good option to consider and don't take much time to research and submit to.

If your news merits a press release or media alert, I also recommend whipping up a blog post that corresponds to the news. You should link to the press release within the blog post, but the post itself should be a more informal and condensed version of the news to get ultimate traction from it.

If your news does not merit a press release or media alert, still write a blog post. Your customers might care about what you want to say, and you don't have to worry about newsworthiness on your own blog. Sharing is caring when it comes to your blog!

In my digital kit (have I mentioned it's available for purchase at my website?), I've included a flowchart that will help you decide whether to use a press release, a media alert or a blog post. If you could use a bit of extra hand-holding in this area, I encourage you to visit me there and check it out.

Here are some of my newswire-pro's favorite tips for start-ups when it comes to writing a solid press release (in his own words, with bolding courtesy of me to accentuate the parts I really hope you pay attention to):

- *Don't be lazy. Seventy to 80 percent of your time should go into the headline and first sentence. **Understand who your audience is and who the journalists are that you're targeting**.*
- *Have some perspective. Nobody cares that you just hired someone (unless they are a common name in the industry).*

Nobody cares about most general corporate happenings. They do care about why your announcement will impact the industry the media covers, the industry the consumer is in, etc. **We used to tell B2C companies all the time that a product announcement should focus in on how that product will help that runner go faster, or that traveler sleep better, etc.**

- **Aim for maximum impact in 10-15 seconds.** *This is how much time the average web page visitor gives a page before moving on. Guess what a press release is? A web page. Also, offer a link to a related page where there is more relevant content to support the release.*

- *Don't pack multiple themes into one release, and don't expect one release to work for media and for consumers.* **They serve two different purposes and require two different styles.**

- **Know what your outcomes should be.** *Do you want the release to be findable for consumers or media? Do you want it to generate some links? What happens if someone clicks? Is your website set up to monitor for those clicks? Are you trying to only get interviews? Is the page you are taking someone to set up to drive some form of action or value? All of these things are key. Hyperlinks are beneficial within a release, just so long as you're strategic with them. Make them count and do not bury them far down in the release.*

- **You need to personalize every press release.** *You have a tech audience? Use their language, be succinct, use bullets to convey key points and get them to a page where they can learn more. Want a journalist response? Know what matters to journalists covering that space and write with an angle that fits the need. Demonstrate a reason for them to care.*

Before we move on to newswires, I wanted to take a second to mention formatting. Press releases must adhere to AP style and are supposed to follow a basic outline to be taken seriously. I include a press release "template" in my digital kit, which shows you how to format a release properly. You, of course, will need to personalize it yourself, but it will at least help you get the formatting started on the right foot.

One piece of formatting I wanted to note is the boilerplate, which is basically the synopsis of your company that sits at the end of a release. This should be written in the third person, include a brief overview of what your company does and your value proposition, state where you're located and give your website address, along with any social media links you'd like interested parties to visit. Here's an example:

Handmade Treasures is a children's toy shop based in Austin, Texas. It was founded to fulfill the mission of making safe and developmentally appropriate toys affordable for parents everywhere. All toys are non-toxic, BPA-free and proudly made by hand in the USA. For more information, please visit us at <insert website link> or follow us on Twitter <insert twitter handle/link>.

Now, onto newswires!

THE NITTY-GRITTY ABOUT NEWSWIRES

If I had a dollar for every time someone asked me to explain how newswire services work, it's safe to say I'd have a LOT of $1 bills. For whatever reason, this process is one giant enigma to most people. If you're one of the 99.2 percent who are confused and daunted by news distribution companies, you're in luck. I'm here to demystify the whole kit and caboodle for you.

First of all, before you understand how they work today, it's important to grasp how newswires of old functioned. Before mainstream web accessibility, "the wire" was a direct news feed into an editorial system that acted as the de facto source of corporate issued news. Additionally, the process to get content digitized and out on the wire was more difficult than it is today so the content was "better."

So, that was then, and this is now (brilliant insight, I know). Today, the sad reality is that there is a lot of bad content on the web in general. Using a newswire service to distribute a targeted, well-written press release can be a great way to cut through the noise and grab the attention of buyers and journalists alike. The press release still serves an exceptionally vital role in promoting what a company is doing while also making its content available via search for journalists who are writing stories and looking for content that may not be a part of a "breaking" news cycle.

In a nutshell, how does a newswire work? It inserts a piece of content into thousands of places online all at once. Some people claim journalists don't even read press releases anymore, but that's just not true. What you do need to be cautious about, though, are the cheap services that declare they can get you a ton of value for far less cash than the most well known newswires can. As the saying goes, if it sounds too good to be true, it is. These services just reinforce the cycle of businesses frequently putting out bad content and further cluttering the web.

The legitimate newswires with which I am most familiar (and consequently endorse) include:
1. PR Newswire
2. Business Wire
3. Marketwired
4. GlobeNewswire

The benefit of using a true premium service is that the higher cost generally means that companies will not pump and dump like many do on free services or cheap services, and there is a higher editorial standard on the larger services (or an editorial standard, period). Consumers and journalists and bloggers start their searches in search engines. Think about what people will be searching for and compelled by when they are scanning through search results or editorial headline flows. Eye tracking shows that people's eyes stick to the left side of the screen and that they skim through results, which makes the headline and the first graph (the part that appears under the headline) so vital.

Bad content will be bad anywhere. Good content paired with a solid newswire can be very, very powerful. Use a cheap wire service and expect cheap results.

Here are a few specific mistakes to avoid making with your press releases:
- Making it all about your company (an ego-play)

- Settling for bad writing
- Failing to add value or showcase the bigger picture of what an announcement actually means

The key to remember is: value first, brand second.

A few final thoughts from my newswire aficionado, especially for start-ups using PR...

- *Don't be cheap on marketing and PR. Use a wire* (Rebecca's note: use a wire IF you have something important enough to say). *If you put out high-quality releases semi-regularly, you increase the likelihood that journalists will have heard about you or your company and may be more receptive to giving you coverage.*
- *Use a good newswire service.*
- *Always use a state distribution.*
- *Always add some compelling photo or video (no faces or logos). This should be something of value, with a caption that tells the story in case the caption/multimedia element was seen away from the press release.*
- *Keep it to 500 words or less.*
- *Remember to link out to relevant content.*
- *Negotiate a flat rate.* (Rebecca's note: Some newswires have switched to a fixed rate across the board, but some still determine cost based on your word count.) *Say you want 10 state releases and 10 multimedia assets for a flat rate equal to 500 words (but with a 600-700 word grace allotment). Ask for 10-20 percent off of that rate. You'll get it. Then you have a budget that you can be sure of.*
- *Use a media monitoring service to listen to what is being said about your brand, and to ID the reporters and bloggers who cover your company's industry. This will help you know what vernacular to use, what topics are important, what angles to take, etc.*
- *Ask the newswire for input on headlines and drafts. They see more headlines in a day than most people see in a year.*
- *Remember who else reads press releases: Consumers! Buyers! Potential customers! Write with perspective and a human voice, and the press release can be as valuable as any other form of content.*

THEN, once the release is live....

- *It can be searchable in perpetuity. If you did your homework and wrote for your audience and not the brand, it should be something someone searches for down the road.*
- *You can customize emails to specific media pros and include a link in the email about why the release will matter to them (DON'T do email blasts to journalists and expect returns. Just like with other forms of content, it's important to know what each media pro writes about, what each of their angles is and customize accordingly).*
- *You can drive people to the release via social media.*
- *It can be stumbled upon across hundreds of sources.*

I wholeheartedly subscribe to (and echo) all of my generous friend's advice! I also wanted to add that newswires are constantly changing their processes, products and services. Keep an eye out for new, innovative offerings that could help you. Just as an example, I recently talked with a sales representative from Marketwired, who explained the company's "Influencer Management" platform. Basically, this service runs several grand a year (although they wouldn't divulge exact numbers), and identifies and aggregates the influencers who are most applicable to you, your company and your industry. I haven't personally used it before, but it sounds like a tool that could help a start-up save a lot of time and hone in on the people they should spend their time talking to if influencers are a key part of their strategy. But, it is also costly so the potential benefit in terms of ROI must be weighed.

And just to be clear – I'm not singling out Marketwired as the one to use, but I am recommending that you look into the particulars of each newswire and decide on one that fits your specific needs. If you have questions, ask the newswire representatives. Yes, they want to sell you, but they can also be great sources of information. And as my colleague mentioned, keep asking questions once you're signed up with a service. Your account representative can give you solid guidance on headlines, verbiage, lengths and distribution.

HOW MUCH TECHNOLOGY DO YOU NEED?

While technology has been sweeping across industries of all shapes and sizes for the last several years to an incredible degree, public relations is a field which historically had not caught up. Sure, newswires use tech tools, but public relations agencies haven't been as up to speed. Part of the reason for this is that PR systems didn't really exist until recent years (at least not great ones).

My former boss, who founded the agency I was with for several years, saw a need for technology in PR and has created a thriving business around a PR software called Iris. This isn't something that you, the start-up, would use, but I'm mentioning it because it's a move in the right direction for PR in general. It's a shift toward being able to more adequately measure the impact of public relations and actually provide corresponding metrics, which was previously unheard of. Agencies and in-house PR teams at larger brands can use a tool like this to manage and measure PR initiatives.

But, what about you? Is technology or measurement of your homegrown PR efforts something that you even need? The honest answer is yes, but not to a large extent. In the early stages of your company, you don't need fancy tools or impressive software systems. Your budget is tight, and so is your time, so you need to be able to quickly gather whether what you do is making a ripple among prospects and customers or not.

For this section, I asked my former boss for her opinion on the best way a start-up can use technology in conjunction with PR, since she's a deeply entrenched leader in the field. I loved her answer. She told me that Google has to be your friend early on. She said it's imperative you get familiar with Google analytics, and pay attention to how long visitors are spending on your site and where they're converting. If you get a media placement, you should automatically get in the habit of reviewing your analytics so you know if it drove a spike in website traffic. It's not super sophisticated, but the blunt reality is that Google analytics is the most important piece of technology you can use as you grow your business.

Part VII: **Content: So You Want to be in Magazines**

By now you get how to manage a compelling blog, could rock a media interview like a pro and know how to write a high-quality press release that you are even starting to understand how to distribute. There couldn't possibly be anything left to this PR hoopla, could there be? Sorry, pals. There is – and it's a behemoth called "content."

Content is a term that means "material." Literally, it's that simple. While a great majority of the content we focus on in PR is written (i.e. blog posts or articles), the label also encompasses things like podcasts and videos. It's basically a vehicle by which you can establish your own credibility or share valuable insight.

Content is one of those modern terms that often leaves the smartest of people somewhat dumbstruck. While most people understand what content refers to, the confusion often surrounds how a business should create and use it. This is a mystery to those outside of PR and marketing, but it's important to understand because the PR industry (and business in general) is largely becoming a content machine. The prevalence of the web and the nearly infinite outlets through which companies and experts can share their thoughts have made it so publishing well-written material is an integral part of doing business. Let me break this down for you so no more questions linger.

CONTRIBUTED ARTICLES

Since we already covered blog posts and press releases, there are three main types of content I'd like to zero in on: contributed articles, profile pieces and white papers.

First, let me clear up a common misconception that applies to articles. As we've established, you will work with a variety of press, but most of them will produce online content. There's a somewhat commonly held belief out there that stories printed in a physical magazine carry more weight with audiences or somehow matter more than those published digitally, but that's a fallacy. In all actuality, most people are consuming their information online. If you end up landing some coverage or a contributed article, it's every bit as important if it's only published digitally. And if it also goes in print? Cool. Cut it out, frame it and hang it on your wall (I'm not joking)!

Moving on... Since we know that people today are voracious for knowledge, and often like to self-teach, articles are a unique opportunity to tap into that hunger. When you, Businessperson Extraordinaire, write an article that gets published by a publication, you have contributed content. So, in the industry, we literally call these types of articles "contributed content" (aren't we clever?). Here's how this process works.

For our pretend scenario du jour, let's say you're an expert on public speaking. You've been a successful speaker in your own career and now the bulk of your business is dedicated to teaching others how to do the same for themselves. Even though you've led both notable keynotes and smaller speaking sessions, you're facing a credibility problem. People don't know who you are and the ones who *are* aware of you don't think you're as much of an authority on the subject as you do. Ouch.

Well, m'dear, it's time for you to consider contributing some content! And why is this? Because contributed content can go a long way in validating your expertise and raising your standing. It helps to position you as a "thought leader." In this play situation, you would first want to think about your core audience. Maybe your ideal client is a solopreneur who runs some sort of consulting business. Great. Next, you'll think about what sort of information those imaginary perfect clients would seek. In this case, they'd probably want information about sales, business and productivity. Once you have an idea of the subject matter, you can then do a little research to find some publications. In this hypothetical instance, you could use search terms like "business magazines," "top sales publications," or "productivity and business." Cull through what you find, then make a list of 10-15 target publications to start with.

Note: While a vast audience reads major publications like *The Wall Street Journal*, *Forbes* and *The New York Times*, I encourage you NOT to start with these. This is because placing contributed content in these outlets is incredibly challenging, whereas industry publications are more apt to accept your work.

If you're struggling to find the magazines that you want to go after, one idea is to poll your current clients informally. This is probably best done over the phone or in-person, as a casual question posed at the tail end of a conversation. "Thanks for the call, Judy. Real quickly, I wanted to ask you a question if you don't mind. Are there any magazines you regularly read?" If your customer rattles off the name of a publication (or two), this can help you figure out where to start.

Once you have that list of 10-15 publications, visit the websites for each one. While you don't want to rule a magazine out simply because of a lackluster digital presence, a terrible website is a telltale sign that a publication may not be worth your time. If it's a decent website, look for a section on "advertising" or a section that says "media kit." You can usually find out the standard circulation (i.e. how many people subscribe to this magazine) and get a feel for the demographics of readers, which will help you decide if writing here is worth your time.

After some online research, you will probably have whittled down your list of 10-15 publications to more like eight to ten. Your next job is to find the masthead. This is the area that, in a printed magazine, lives just a few pages after the cover and lists out the names and titles of the people who work for the magazine. Online, this information is usually buried somewhere. It could be in a "contact" section, an "about us" page or even somewhere more obscure.

After you find the masthead, you should identify a person with the title "editor" or "managing editor." This is who you want to contact before going further. If you can't find this person on the site, find someone whose email you can get your hands on. If you find the name of the person in one of these roles, but their email isn't listed, get creative with searching. If your only hope is to use a webform that's displayed for contacting the publication, go ahead and use it.

At this point, you should create a media list. This is a term for a spreadsheet that includes all the information about any members of the press you'd like to target. Include each person's name, title, email address, publication and beat. If you'd like, separate the list into "top tier" and "second tier" media entities. Top tier outlets are those that have a high circulation and are often general business magazines and household names. Second tier outlets are often industry publications and smaller outlets. It can help to parse these out because then you can set goals for yourself as to how many media hits you'd like to have in top tier publications and how many you're aiming for in second tier publications. Ultimately, though, frame your media list however you'd like (and if you're wondering, yes – there is a media list framework available in my digital kit).

Anyway, back to pitches. Your note to an editor or managing editor should be something like this:

Subject: Quick question re: contributed content

Hi Betty,

I'm reaching out to ask if you accept contributed content? If so, I would love to have one of my articles considered.

Some topics I'd be happy to write about include:
- "Public Speaking 101: Skills Even the Most Accomplished Leaders Should Brush Up On"
- "Live Technical Difficulties? Use them to Fuel the Best Speech of your Career"
- "Your Bio is your Foot in the Door: Write one that will Captivate from within any Program Book"

Do you think any of these topics would be a good fit for your readers? I run my own company, Public Speaking Elite, and have been teaching people how to speak in public for the past 10 years. I would love to help your readers do the same. Could you please let me know if there might be room for an article from me?

Thank you,
Rebecca

This email is polite and brief, but gives just enough information that Betty can quickly decide if she wants to entertain the idea of a contributed article from this person. Three quick tips on the topic ideas you propose:

1. They should fit into the subject matter of content that is regularly featured in the publication you're pitching.

2. The headlines you give should be interesting! You can create these and worry about fulfilling a full article about them later. Just the headlines are enough for now.

3. Do a quick search on the website to make sure no previous stories have run in this publication that are identical to what you're offering.

You can use this same email (and the same topics) to send to all of your target publications. If you happen to be lucky enough that four or more magazines bite on your offer, just let the fourth one know that you've since committed the other topics to different publications, but have a new headline you think would be perfect for them (and then let them know what that is). Odds are, you might hear back from one or two of these publications and won't ever have to worry about offering the same story to multiple outlets. Just never write the same (or a very similar) article for different sites. Be honest in the initial stages and come up with new material for one publication if there are two that want the same topic.

One more note about contributed content. A vast majority of publications only accept articles that are unbiased. This means you have to write from an objective point of view, and almost never can mention your company. Readers will be able to see your company's name and click through to your website when they check out the bio next to your byline (the part that says, "By: Rebecca Hasulak"). Don't worry, they'll see your company name and find you if they're interested. But, don't expect a publication to publish an article you write if you sneakily try to slip in some advertorial copy about your own business if they've asked you to keep the piece vendor-neutral! It's best to always stick to their editorial guidelines, which you can ask for once an editor expresses interest in an article from you.

Editorial Calendars

If you are struggling to land an article (whether it's a profile piece about your company or a contributed piece of content), consider turning to a publication's editorial calendar. Basically, this is exactly what it sounds like – a calendar that keeps publications organized with their content and advertising. If you've been paying attention, this is pretty much like what you will soon have going for your company blog.

Just like titles and names and email addresses can sometimes be hard to find on publications' websites, finding editorial calendars can also pose a challenge. Sometimes magazines will have a calendar that relates to advertising, other times it will refer to editorial opportunities and still other times it will include both. Any of these versions is useful to you. Look for the editorial calendar in any section that offers information about advertising or boasts a media kit. This is where it's most likely to be found. Don't despair if you can't find one; many outlets do not make them publicly available.

If you can find a publication that does share its editorial calendar, give yourself a high-five! This insider look at the planning of a publication can work greatly in your favor. The calendar should include some sort of smorgasbord that lays out the sections of the magazine, what specific topics will be centered on each month and the "ad close" and "editorial close." You will want to pay close attention to the topics and the editorial close.

Search through these for the year ahead, and write down which subjects tie in to your expertise. If there's a focus on non-GMO foods in a health magazine scheduled for May, that's something that an organic foods company might want to start thinking about in January (or even earlier). As soon as you see a topic that fits what you can write about, reach out to the editor and pitch a story idea or contributed article. Explain why you have expertise in the area and how your article will be a great fit for that month's concentration. Also, be sure to take note of the editorial close, which is the date by when the publication expects to have all of its content delivered.

The leg up you have if you pitch contributed content according to editorial calendars is that the publication is already planning on zeroing on the topic you know you can write about. So, it'll just be a matter of whether your proposed headline is interesting, and whether they still have room for an additional piece.

Writing a Worthy Article

While I am an earnest advocate of doing your own PR (hence this entire book), I will never suggest you sludge your way through writing. As a nerdy writing enthusiast and self-proclaimed grammar freak, I believe that English is a beautiful language, and that written communication can be a great gift. If you don't enjoy writing or question your abilities, you might not want to be the person who writes the public-facing content for your company. Please don't break my heart like that! Just like there's a reason that certain people are CEOs, there's a reason certain people are writers.

There are three main areas I believe are crucial to writing good articles: Clarity, concision and accuracy in spelling and grammar. If you're confident you can handle all areas, feel free to write blog posts, social media posts, articles, press releases and the like for your business. But if you're missing any of those three parts, I'd encourage you to designate this writing to somebody else (more on outsourcing writing in the next section).

Here's why each of the areas of writing I mentioned matter:

Clarity
If you want to write compelling articles, you need to be upfront with your reader about what he or she is going to get from taking time to read your words. I suggest three ways of doing this:
1. Write an accurate, catchy headline. Note that I did not say campy, kitschy or cutesy for your headline – but rather catchy. Your headline should leave no doubt about what your article includes, and it should do so in a moderately creative way. Don't be abstract or artsy, or you'll lose potential readers. Be practical and clear. "Stop Wasting your Life with These Time Management Tricks" is a solid headline. "I Don't Wanna Wait for my Life to be Over: A Lesson in Time Management" is creative, but way too long and bordering on campy. "Oh Time, Where Art Thou?" is just silly and does not tell me why I should read this article.
2. Engage with a strong introduction. Most people will read a few sentences of your article and either continue reading, or abandon ship and wander elsewhere in the digital universe. Keep them reading by being relatable, clear (yes, still!) and interesting.

3. Break up the copy. Use subheadings or bullet points wherever appropriate. This gives the eye a more pleasing, organized piece to look at and makes your mind think that reading it from start to finish is a doable feat.

Get to the point!
This one just about crushed me when I started in PR. I was that girl who looooved being extra descriptive and using big, long, pretty words in my writing. I honestly wasn't trying to show off; I just love the English language and piecing together beautifully orchestrated sentences was (or should I say *is*) fun for me. When I started writing as an intern at a PR agency, my boss and co-workers immediately stopped me in my tracks. Sometimes they sugarcoated it and said things like, "Oh, Rebecca, you're such an academic writer! You have a wonderful vocabulary." And other times, they cut to the chase and basically said I was in the throes of a debilitating habit and needed to cut it out.

As painful as it was to learn to write in a different style (and bid adieu to those gorgeous words that most people do not use in normal conversation), this was a priceless lesson for me to learn. I'm so grateful that these PR pros held my hand and were honest with me about what works in PR writing – and what does not.

Sometimes you'll hear people say things like, "use $0.10 words" or "stop using $0.50 words." I don't like trite phrases like this, but the underlying point is valid. The gist of this is: Do not use large or confusing words when a simpler word works just as well. You might think using the word "emblematize" makes you sound smart or that the word "illuminate" sounds so pretty in the sentence before you. But, if the word "demonstrate" will convey your point better to more people, then use it instead.

Your goal is to make your writing conversational, so think about the words that real humans naturally use in their interactions. You want your words to paint a clear picture, not create confusion. And you also want to say what you mean to say as quickly as you can. Attention spans today are shockingly short, and no one wants to waste time wading through flowery language and circuitous trains of thought to get to the heart of your message.

Reflection on you and your brand

You might be the type of person who doesn't think typos matter, but oh do they ever! Sure, you can get away with a misspelling or a missing comma here or there, but if mistakes are frequent, you're doing your brand an incredible disservice. Your written communications are a direct reflection of the standards you hold yourself to – personally and professionally. Errors translate into laziness or stupidity, even if they're really just the result of ignorance or being in a rush. Try your best to avoid consistent typos, grammatical errors or even inconsistencies in what you produce. One typo every once in a blue moon is not a big deal. But, little typos sprinkled here and there all add up to an image of sloppiness, carelessness and lack of quality.

Have a writer look over every piece of written material that will be public-facing. Use the best writer on your team or find a freelancer to edit your work. And even if your best writer is writing everything, still make sure each piece passes before one or two additional sets of eyes before it leaves your walls. The most competent writers are still human and will miss things that a fresh perspective will spot. I believe in this so much, and I assure you I have had plenty of my own Kool-Aid to drink. For this book, I've hired a highly skilled editor to comb over every word with a fine-tooth comb to check for errors and polish the final piece. So, please believe me this is important.

I've heard some people say that English mistakes don't matter to the majority of people. But, even if many people don't care about mistakes, many do. I can't tell you how many times I've seen an ad promoting a "sneak peak" (it should be "sneak pe_e_k") and I've instantly lost respect for the brand. I'm sure that makes me sound like a self-righteous jerk, but there's really no excuse for elementary mistakes like that. Your brand deserves better.

Finally, I recommend that companies write according to AP style. This is the standard set of rules that the Associated Press follows in its writing, and it's what press releases are expected to adhere to. Many publications also require their contributed content to fit AP style standards. Because of this, I like to keep all written materials consistent with AP style so that all of your written works maintain uniformity and meet journalistic quality. The one exception is for actual books, since Chicago style is the generally accepted style to follow for books and I also think you can have some freedom of expression in your blog posts. But, otherwise, please stick to AP style.

You can either buy an updated AP stylebook online or can purchase a subscription to the digital version, whichever you prefer. You'll find things like "%" should always be written as "percent" and "web" should be "Web." Little things like this will be spotted by journalists who write in this style day in and day out, so just make it easy and make this your mainstay. If you want to check out some of the most common mistakes made with AP style, I've included a quick guide in my digital kit (yep – available for purchase at my website).

If you can handle these prongs of writing yourself, super. If not, don't stress! It's not worth it to try to forge your way through written materials. Good writing cannot be faked. You can find freelance writers pretty easily either through personal referrals or through services like Upwork (my personal recommendation) or Freelancer, and they will be worth their weight in gold. Be sure to check their career backgrounds so you know they actually know what they're doing, and that their rate looks fair.

So, what happens if you write an article that gets published by a digital magazine? A.k.a. you've contributed content? Yay you!

First, enjoy the moment! You're now on your way to becoming a "thought leader!" Second, be sure to share the piece through your own personal social channels and your company's social channels. Third, check it regularly to see if readers have left comments. I highly recommend engaging with people who have left you comments, whether they're good or bad. If they're bad, keep your own words positive. You never want to leave anything negative in your wake online. Hopefully all your comments will be great ones though!

Ghostwriting

I still remember when I first started in PR and how my innocent beliefs were slowly shattered bit by bit. Okay, so I'm being a little dramatic. But before walking along this career path, I never thought that a piece of writing could have been written by someone other than its purported author. Quotes in press releases? Oh, those were definitely the exact words spoken by the person being quoted. Articles in magazines? Sure thing, those are absolutely written by the author whose name is displayed in the byline. Right? I mean... how deceptive if that isn't the case... how wrong...

But alas, not everything attributed to a certain person is in fact written by that person. I would allege that at least half of all online content (if not a good deal more) is ghostwritten. This basically means that someone else wrote the article or blog post, and then a different person got all the glory. Sounds pretty awful, right? I thought so too.

However, there really is a reason for this and I have come to be more accepting of the practice. I'd be lying if I said I didn't actively contribute to this underworld of writing sins, either, as at least 95 percent of everything I've written now lives online proudly under other people's names. But here's why ghostwriting works and is, dare I say, necessary. Many business leaders don't have the time, energy, skill or desire to write the content that they need to in order to establish themselves as "thought leaders." Instead of holding this against them, consider the fact that ghostwriting allows them (and you) an opportunity to share your ideas with the world without losing even more of your precious time or getting hung up on sentence flow and spelling errors.

In my career, the majority of ghostwriting I've done has been on behalf of some wickedly smart people. The "author" of the piece would usually have at least a small part in coming up with the topic idea, and then I would typically interview him or her to get a brain dump of all thoughts that should be conveyed within the piece. Then, I would write the whole article and take it back to the "author" for review. So in the end, it was always this individual's thoughts being shared – just via the vehicle of my shaping, writing and refining. When you think of it this way, it really does make sense.

If I'm being honest, I do wish that there was less ghostwriting in the world and more authentic pieces coming straight from the mouths (well, hands) of experts. But this practice isn't going away anytime soon. And as you get busier and busier in your business, you very well might benefit from using the services of a ghostwriter. When push comes to shove, it's just a little naughty – and a lot rewarding.

PROFILE PIECES

In the prior section about media interviews, I briefly mentioned that a conversation with the press could lead to a profile piece. I'd like to explain what that is, and how it works. Essentially, a profile piece is an article in which your company is profiled (don't you love when something is exactly what it sounds like?). This means that a reporter would be the one writing the story and, as opposed to most forms of contributed content, the story is actually about you and your company.

A reporter is likely to write such a piece if your company has been making waves in the industry (or larger business scene) for one reason for another. If you've closed a big funding round and are able to hire a large number of new employees, for example, this could be something of interest to a local business reporter. To secure an interview with a member of the press and open yourself up to the opportunity of having a profile piece written about you, you need to still send a pitch – this time about yourself and your company specifically. Look for people with the title "reporter" because, unlike an editor, they will be the ones writing this type of story.

WHITE PAPERS

Another type of content is something called a "white paper." I remember the first time I heard someone use the term in a business meeting, and I started laughing. I honestly thought he was making a joke because, obviously, all paper is white! I wish I was making this up, but I was really that naïve! I like to think I'm a touch more savvy than I was back then, but at the very least I am now well acquainted with white papers.

A white paper is basically a long-form piece of content. The word count ranges vary depending on who you ask, but these documents usually are double to triple the length of a standard article. This type of piece can be useful in very technical fields, or when you need to delve into nuanced aspects of a particular subject. They can also be helpful if your audience is one that needs a good deal of education about your value proposition, the market you're in or something else related to what you do.

I recommend finding a skilled writer to help you bring these meaty beasts to life, because they turn out best when produced by someone familiar with the format and function. If you put together a white paper, you can use it on your website as a way to capture leads ("enter your email address here and we'll send you a free report on the 12 benefits of eating cupcakes!") or elsewhere in your marketing efforts. But, I would not pitch a white paper to the press. Unless you speak with a journalist who specifically says she is dying to get her hands on an in-depth paper like this, keep it to yourself and your own marketing purposes. Most press do not dally in white papers, and even fewer consider publishing them.

A final note on white papers: If you do create any, you can use them for a long time! The extensive content contained within their pages can be repurposed in many ways. Extract material to inspire blog posts, copy and paste key points to live on as social media posts – and so on. If you go to the trouble of getting deep with white papers, you should definitely maximize the final result.

PITCHING THE PRESS

As with everything in PR, any measure you take should be tied directly to a larger goal. Sometimes these goals are more overarching (like generating general brand awareness) and other times they're more specific (like getting 20 new leads from a conference). I want you to think about this mindset when it comes to pitching the press.

In the prior section, I gave you a sample email to use as a reference point for securing contributed articles. In this section, I'll briefly outline some ideas for structuring emails you use to ask for other things you want from the media. Keep in mind that you can offer a phone call anytime you want to book a meeting, or you can suggest an in-person meeting if you're located near the person or expecting to attend the same event. You'll notice there are some definite themes among the following emails, and that this is really not that difficult. But, it'll hopefully clarify the process for you and help you see how approachable this all can be. (Side note: The stat I use in the second pretend email below is completely fabricated, so don't fact-check me! Your emails should include real, corroborated data if you make any such references).

Asking for a Background Briefing

Hi Brenda,

I noticed that you're going to be at the Event Planners United Conference coming up next month. I'm going too, and I wanted to see if you might have a half hour free to grab coffee with me one of the days we're there?

I've been following what you write and really connected with your recent piece about the emotional aspect of event planning. I own my own event business, Magical Moments, and have grown from a one-person shop to a fully staffed team of 15 in just two years. I'd love to talk with you, hear more about what upcoming stories you have planned and give you some more background on me and my company. Is there a day and time that's good for you for this?

Thank you for the consideration,
Rebecca

Asking for an Interview

Hi Paul,

I'm reaching out to introduce myself to you and ask if you might be willing to have a quick call with me sometime in the next week? I'm familiar with your articles, and I have noticed you've written a lot recently about marketing automation. My company, Modern Marketing, just launched a new product that complements marketing automation software perfectly, and I'm eager to tell you about it.

I'd also love to be a resource for you on any future stories about the market and current trends, like the news that 42 percent of marketing automation users have abandoned their systems within the first month due to insufficient training. I have so much to say on the topic, and I think your readers might be interested to hear my take!

Anyway, is there a good time in the next week that we could jump on a call and have a quick conversation?

Looking forward to it,
Rebecca

Pitching a Story Idea Based on an Editorial Calendar Topic

Hi Jamie,

I noticed that the June issue of your magazine is focused on personal finance. As the owner of R&R Financial Planning, I wanted to see if you might be interested in a contributed article from me for this section?

Some topics I could write about include:
- *"Budgeting for the Impulse Buyer"*
- *"A Marriage between a Spender and a Saver: How to Make it Work"*
- *"Four Tips to Never Take on Debt Again"*

Do you think your readers might want to read one of these pieces? Please let me know, and I'd be happy to write the full article and send it over for your review.

Thanks so much,
Rebecca

Finally, I wanted to mention something about follow-up. If you send a note to a reporter and don't hear back, please resist the urge to harangue them until they respond to you. In the interest of common courtesy, I recommend waiting a full week (or about four or five business days) before following up to your first email. When you do follow up, try using a subject line like "Getting back to you re: proposed story idea" or "Re: proposed story idea" or "Help with proposed story idea?" These subject lines are the ones I've experienced the most success with in my own pitching quests. And, this should go without saying, but be just as kind and inquisitive in your second email as you were in the first. I've had many journalists thank me for sending a follow-up note because they truly hadn't seen my first one (or had flagged it for later and forgot to get around to it).

PREPARATION IS YOUR PAL: HOW TO PACK YOUR MEDIA KIT

So, now you're jazzed about pitching the press on contributed content ideas, angles for profile pieces, opportunities for interviews and beyond. But, what happens when a journalist writes you back? What if he asks for you something? What if you don't have it, or can't get it in time?

This is where the media kit part of the puzzle comes in. The media will generally ask you for some very basic things to help them either publish your story or write one of their own. Most PR agencies will have all of these items neatly ready in advance, in a digital folder they'll refer to as a media kit. So, here's what goes into this fun little folder.

There are two different kinds of media kits, one that publications offer and one that you should have. The one that publications have includes information that helps advertisers and other members of the media learn more about their magazine and readership. If you were paying attention during the section on editorial calendars, you might remember that this variety of media kit usually includes an editorial calendar too.

The other type of media kit, however, is one that I want to cover. It's the one that you should have prepared for your own company. This is another one of those things that is simple to pull together, but crucial for any solid PR program. This is what your media kit should include:
- Headshots of all the senior leaders in your company
- Bios for every leader in your company
- High-res images of your logo and your product if possible
- A messaging document that includes your company's value proposition in varying lengths intended for varying audiences.

You might be thinking, "Wow, that's not hard at all. I could easily pull that together if I'm ever asked for this information. There's no point in handling it right now and it's not a priority." But, the reality is, things in digital publishing move quickly. If you get a reporter on the line for a phone call or expressing interest in you for a profile piece or commentary on breaking news, you're going to need to send over whatever that person needs nearly instantly. Sometimes they'll give you a grace period of a couple days or if you're very lucky, maybe a week. But, more often than not, journalists will expect whatever materials they need within a few hours. After all, they have deadlines to meet.

Your company bios should be just about four to five sentences in length. They should briefly explain your title and what you do at your current company, a brief encapsulation of your past career history and anything else that is noteworthy to your current line of work (like if you're also an author or regular speaker). This is not the place to plug how much you love chili cheese fries or that you've kayaked in the San Juan Islands 12 times. If you're crazy about those little interesting tidbits, they can go in your company bios on your website if you feel like they add some personality to your brand. But, the bios in your media kit are supposed to be of a more serious nature that let the publication and its readers know why you're credible to speak about the topic at hand.

Within your media kit, I also recommend including a one to two sentence version of your bio because sometimes publications will request a shortened version instead. Depending on how the outlet formats its posts, your longer bio might be used on an author profile page, while your shorter bio might be used next to your byline. Having the longer and shorter versions easily accessible makes it very easy for you to just copy and paste whichever is preferred and send it on over to the editor lickety-split.

When it comes to headshots, a lot of companies balk at this. They think that there is no reason to have professional pictures done. They say they'll just snap a picture with their iPhone or use that one really great picture from back when they were skiing the Appalachian Mountains. While I'm sure your selfie game is strong (trust me, I hate myself for even saying that) and that your ski pictures are way too fun, I highly recommend having professional pictures done. Again, these are a representation of your brand. If the pictures tied to your articles seem hokey or grainy or have you out in nature doing something sporty or otherwise that doesn't relate to the topic at hand, you're just going to look disjointed and unprofessional.

I know firsthand how expensive professional pictures can be, but there are a few ways to get around this. First, you can do some digging online (or by calling a photography school) to find budding photographers who have good equipment and editing capabilities but don't have the experience to be able to charge outrageous rates. Another way to do it is to ask a friend who you know is good at photography and see if you can get a discount. A third way is to do it yourself. This last one, of course, leaves you the open to mistakes and poor quality, but sometimes there isn't another way.

I know I joked about the iPhone camera before, but cellular cameras really are pretty high quality and not terrible as a last-ditch resort. If you absolutely cannot afford to hire somebody professional to take your pictures, then at least get similar looking pictures against the same background. Less busy backgrounds are better, like a plain white or dark background. I wouldn't opt for a color background and would stick to the more typical whites, grays and blacks. Color can be distracting and can be unflattering on certain skin tones and hair colors.

Also, make sure there are no shadows where you're shooting and that there are no fluorescent lights overhead. Natural light is best if you can swing it. Take a bunch of photos and find the best one. Then, use a photo-editing app like FaceTune or something similar to make sure it looks polished. One word of caution, however, with photo editing apps: practice restraint. A lot of people try to use the very fancy editing tools and often end up with pictures that look extremely unprofessional and cheesy. Refrain from making your teeth shockingly white, trying to thin out your face or making your ears look smaller than they are (I'm onto your tricks). Use photo-editing tools simply for lighting, cropping and doing away with really distracting things like blemishes.

Another tip is to try to get everybody's shots taken within the same frame. This is photography-speak that just means if you shoot one person's headshot from his hips up to his head, do the same with everyone else's. If you want a tighter frame (like shoulders to top of head), then shoot this way for all parties. Do this and shoot against the same background to keep your brand looking consistent. Final note: Most publications are going to want your headshots in a high-res format, so have them prepared and saved this way.

Your headshot and bio are going to be the most frequently requested items out of your media kit, but a publication may also want an image of your company logo. This is usually more if they're going to be doing a profile piece rather than if you're contributing an article. You will also need to have your logo handy for something like putting out a press release over the wire so it should be easily accessible at all times.

Last, but not least, I recommend having a good messaging document that includes descriptions of your value proposition. The reason you should have multiple descriptions that vary in length and by target buyer is because you will want to send over different snapshots for different media. For instance, if you own a denim company and a reporter asks what your company does, you should send over a different description to an industry magazine that targets teens than you would to a business publication that is interested in how you've scaled production. This doesn't have to be complicated. Just jot down a more in-depth overview of what you offer to each buyer group, and then a brief, one-to-two sentence version so you can pull whichever out when appropriate.

Part VIII: **Awards: Hello, Smoke and Mirrors**

Awards are like anything else in PR. They're a tool, nothing more and nothing less. They are something you can use to further your goals.

Awards are funny because, prior to being in PR, they used to seem somewhat magical to me. I would see a "best product" award badge on a website and think, "Ooh, they must be the greatest!" Fast forward to my present self, years after being jaded about the industry (in a nice way), and I see awards and think, "good job, PR department." I may sound cynical, but the businesses that get awards are generally those that know how to – or have PR people who do.

Don't get me wrong – plenty of awards are legitimate and truly recognize great products, services or accomplishments. Businesses don't typically nab them if they're not deserving. But, as with most things in life, awards are also a bit of a game. It's all a bit of smoke and mirrors. Think about it: no matter the award, you're judged against the other people who also submitted entries. But, if you win, it'll look like you earned the recognition OVERALL OUT OF ALL COMPANIES EVER! It sounds silly but most people don't think, "Oh nice, they're the best sales team out of the two whole companies who entered the program." Nope. Most people think, "WOW! I want to deal with an awesome salesperson and this award says they're THE BEST so they really must be!"

So, from this aspect, it's all a bit deceptive (to the award winner's benefit). In addition to this, award programs are usually pay-for-play. They're businesses like anybody else and they want to see just how much you're willing to fork over to get your prize! In a past life (a.k.a. my early teen years), I entered a beauty competition hosted by a sunscreen brand. The program told my mom (who was kind enough to accompany me to this silly thing) that I could be "considered" for the Best Smile, Coolest Hair, Most Fabulous Personality, etc. "extra awards"… for the small, little sum of something like $50 per award. We (well, she) had already paid an entry fee for me for the general competition. But, they had the audacity to say, "Pay us more! And *maybe* your daughter will get another trophy."

The only reason I bring up this experience is because it's exactly how most award companies work. They will charge you for one entry, and then often nickel and dime you for extras. Oh, you want to be judged on three things and not just one? Sure – just pay us three times as much. Ah, you actually want to have a plaque you can put in your office so you can share your win with people? It'll just be a cool $500. And on and on. My point in exposing this side of the business is to ask you to proceed with caution. If you can afford a basic entry fee, then stick to that. Do not agree to additional costs, no matter how tempting they seem. And if even a basic entry fee will cause you to lose sleep or miss payroll, I beg of you to skip the award for now!

So, now that you know some of the ickier parts about awards, let's talk about their benefits. The most obvious one is that double-edged sword we discussed above. While a bit on the deceptive side, you will instantly gain credibility and standing in the eyes of your customers, prospects, peers and competitors when you win an award (or even place as a finalist). This can be very helpful when someone is whittling down their options of who they might want to work with. One well-chosen award could make the difference!

I mentioned that awards are tools, and here's how. You can use them to fill in the areas where your company is weak - or maybe isn't weak, but just wants to be stronger. It's like plugging the holes in a boat that are probably too small to sink the whole thing, but are keeping it from being as afloat as it could be. To use them strategically, you want to consider your upcoming goals.

Here are a few examples:

- Are you looking to attract top talent as you start a big hiring push? A "best places to work" award could raise your level of attractiveness in the eyes of applicants and get you "free" publicity.
- Did you get some bad feedback (or press) about your customer service department and need to do a 180-degree turn on this poor public perception? Submit for a customer service award.
- Having trouble gaining credibility and awareness for your SaaS solution in a highly crowded market? Look into general software or more specific SaaS awards that could

automatically help you to be perceived as a contender in the space.

- Are you trying to get acquired and need to demonstrate your growth? Check out some sales or "fastest-growing companies" type awards.

Hopefully this helps you to see how you can align your bigger picture goals with the awards you enter. Oh, and one side note: Even though I totally bagged on awards programs and their penchant for getting you to shell out cash, there *are* some free ones out there! So, you don't always need to have an awards budget to enter awards if you're careful about which ones you go after.

Once you decide if now is, in fact, the time to pursue awards, the next step is determining what type of award would make the most sense for your brand. I gave several examples above, and I trust you to be able to extrapolate them out to your own situation. So, once you know the type of awards you want to get, where do you find them?

FINDING AND VETTING AWARDS

Ideas to find awards:

1. Look at your competitors' sites (or those you hope to count as your competitors someday) to see what awards they've won.
2. Aim for industry awards first, then the broader, more crowded ones later.
3. Do some digging on the websites of the publications you've identified as ones your target customer is reading. Many awards are sponsored by or tied to magazines.
4. Still need more to choose from? Power up the Google machine. Begin by typing in specific search terms and then getting more vague until you find results. For instance, you want a customer support award for your app. Type "customer support", "award" and "apps." If you don't find applicable results, then try "customer service," "award," "technology." Still nothing? Then try "award" and "business." You're sure to find some results, probably even with the very specific search terms.

How to vet an award:

This is definitely more of a subjective exercise and is not any sort of science. First, go to the awards site. Similarly to how you gauged whether a digital magazine is worth its salt, you should get an immediate sense for whether the awards program is legitimate. You're not looking for the fanciest, most technologically advanced website out there, but you do need to verify that it looks somewhat visually appealing and is comprehensive. In other words, it shouldn't look janky.

Second, find a list of prior winners. Most award sites will have a separate section for this, but if you can't find it, they may have the winners listed in a press release in their press/news section. Still can't find it? Try Googling again (tired of me saying that yet?). Once you have your hands on past winners, you should easily be able to tell if the companies are decent and functioning businesses with which you would be comfortable being in the same company. If there's anything you see that you don't like, "just pass" (as Milton from *Office Space* would say). Your intuition is a strong guide.

Looking at past winners can also give you some insight into whether you'd have a shot at winning the award. If the award costs $350 to apply for and past winners include nothing but Fortune 500 companies, you may want to hold off for another year. But, if you think you can hold your own against the past winners, it's probably a good one to enter.

Third – and this isn't really part of the vetting process – you'll want to look at what's required in an entry. Some award programs ask for financial (or other) information that many companies aren't willing to disclose. It's better to know this upfront before you ever start preparing an entry. And no, don't ask if you can have an exception. I'm usually a proponent of the "always ask" school of thought, but in this case, it's a waste of time. If they say they require something, they require it from *everybody*.

Sometimes, it's hard to access the application or requirements without handing over your social security number and first-born child. Okay, not really, but it can feel that way. A program may ask you to give your name and contact information, and promise to email you the details. Or some programs make you create an account and only grant you access to one page of the application at a time, forcing you to submit answers as you go. They'll hate me for saying this, but in that instance – create a dummy account with ZERO identifying information and submit a fake application so you know what you're working with before ever having to write one word. You could get to the last page and realize they ask you for something you're uncomfortable giving (or simply don't have), and you wasted a bunch of time.

So, get all the requirements first. And then it's time to prepare, baby!

WRITING A WINNING ENTRY

So, now you've established that you have an award worth applying for, and you know what the submission process is going to take. You need to use your best writer (or outsource to a freelancer) for this application. Unless it's a purely tech-based award where the judging panel pokes around your technology and nothing else, your writing is what will seal the deal or kill your odds of winning.

Extra credit/the cherry on top: If there's ever an "optional" section you can fill out, do so! It's not time to get lazy. Or if there's ever a place where you can insert numbers/metrics or anecdotes, be like Nike and just do it! These added pieces of info are like the toppings on a sundae. Sure, vanilla ice cream is delicious as is. But, who would ever choose plain vanilla if you had the option to get vanilla covered with caramel and Reese's? Exactly my point (and for you plain vanilla fanatics, I like you, but I will never understand you). So, all this to say that more *quality* material is always better than less.

As always, let me give you an example of a 'brief' part of a submission two ways. This is a hypothetical photography company submitting for a "Most Creative Use of Lighting" award.

Q: What has your company done to show its creativity with lighting?

A: Our company, Prestige Photography, shows its creativity with lighting every day. We help our clients find unique settings and then capitalize on the time of day to produce interesting shots.

Bleh. I mean, that tells the judging panel, NOTHING. Here's a better answer...

A: As a special occasion photography company, Prestige Photography focuses on using natural light to capture unique images. The silhouettes we get for couples' engagement photos are one of our trademark offerings that have ended up framed in over 160 clients' homes. We also regularly shoot maternity photos in the lighting just after a sunrise, which beautifully showcases the fresh glow of a pregnant mom-to-be. As our client Rachel Robson recently said, "Prestige Photography used natural light and expert techniques to pull out the radiance I feel about my unborn baby. I couldn't have been more pleased!"

Which version would stand out to you more, as a judge? Notice I put in numbers where I could, specific examples and a real client testimonial. A few side notes: Ask your client if you are allowed to use his or her words in an award application before doing so. And only use numbers if they strengthen your case! If you're submitting an application in which the program asks for sales growth and you've only grown by $1K in revenue over a year... that will make you look small. Don't include weak numbers if you don't have to, and it's usually permissible to use percentages instead of numbers if they cast you in a more favorable light.

Another thing: The second example I gave is longer, but better applications are not always longer. Still aim to be as concise as you can while presenting the most strong, real aspects of your company story. Most awards will give you a maximum word count. Don't pad your application with fluff to reach close to that number. Just make sure you stay under the max, and present an eloquent, thoughtfully put-together application.

Finally, once you have a well-prepared award entry, repurpose it! Use the same content (as long as it's applicable) for other award submissions. You'll save yourself time and, if it's a winning entry, you might get a lot of runway out of something you only had to focus on once.

Part IX: **Speaking: If You can Talk, You can Speak – Kind Of**

I'm told there was a time when speaking opportunities were doled out based on merit. While that sounds really great, the truth is that isn't how it works all that much anymore. There are events here and there that actually do choose speakers because of their credentials and the power of what they have to share, but the trend is currently that more and more speaking opportunities are tied to... you guessed it, sponsorship!

I can't even tell you the number of times that I've reached out to an organization to ask about their speaking opportunities and received a response that says something along the lines of, "we still have a few open but all of them are tied to sponsorship! Are you an exhibitor?" This is another one of those dirty little secrets about PR.

Most people go to conferences and events with the nice, happy illusion that speakers are there because they're the most qualified people to be speaking. Not always so. Can you imagine how attendees would feel if they first were shown a spreadsheet with all the speakers' names and the amounts that they have paid to be there? It would really burst their bubble and varnish the perception of grandeur.

But, I certainly don't mean to be all doom and gloom (what, me?). The good news is that most people are not aware of this and even if they are, will still find value in a speaker's presentation as long as it is full of meaningful content. It's kind of like if your VP of operations is also the CEO's daughter. You would definitely cry nepotism at first! But, if she actually was a force to be reckoned with in her job, you would eventually forget about how unfair it was for her to land that position and end up respecting her for what she's doing.

Of course, I have to add in a caveat here because there will be somebody who is sure to point it out. Not all speaking opportunities are based on sponsorship levels and there are still many events that choose their speakers on an even playing field. Even those conferences that require speakers to be exhibitors, still might choose some of their speakers based on merit.

But, one major note with that is that there's also something enormous to be said about name recognition. Most speakers who are paid to speak, rather than who *pay* to speak, are those who have massive followings for some reason or another. Just think about who would draw a bigger crowd – Carrie Underwood or Carrie Unknown? Exactly.

At the end of the day (oh how I hate that cliché), events and conferences are businesses just like anything else. They want to make money and the ways in which they make most of their money are through attendee fees and sponsorship payments. So, their main goal will be to select speakers who have either paid them to exhibit or who will draw in a big crowd and therefore net them more attendee-based profit. Also, the greater the number of attendees, the greater the bidding becomes for advertising options. It's all cyclical, and it all comes back to money.

So, what's a person like you to do, who has great things to say and is starting a valuable business, but has zilch as far as name recognition and no foot in the door with any of these conferences? Worse yet – what's a start-up to do that is strapped for cash and can't afford to exhibit at events, but feels that speaking is an important part of your public approach? Well, my suggestion is that you roll the dice! I know it's not a particularly concrete recommendation, or based in facts or numbers, but you need to start applying as much as you can if you want to land a speaking gig.

While I'm a firm believer in the quote about reaching for the moon and landing among the stars, I also think a healthy dose of pragmatism is important in PR. If you're not Tim Cook or Marissa Mayer, people are likely not going to request your keynote. At least not right now! And while there are plenty of events that you may dream of headlining like TechCrunch Disrupt, these are the types of conferences that are extremely hard to crack even for rising stars in the business world. I would avoid them for now. This isn't to say you have to let go of your dreams, but just table them until you've had a chance to establish a proven track record and gain some notoriety.

In lieu of these, I highly recommend beginning with smaller industry events. And specifically, the ones in your area. After all, you are a start-up that needs to be very conscientious about your budget. You do not need to be spending money traveling to another city and buying airfare, hotel stays, rental cars, meals out, etc.... just to pay somebody to sponsor and speak. It just doesn't make mathematical sense. Look for events in your state. And don't worry – it's okay if there aren't that many to choose from initially. There's a reason that speaking is last in this book. It's because I believe it's what you need to focus on the least as a company in the early stages. Yes, there's benefit. But, this can always wait.

If you struggle to land even an industry speaking gig, don't lose heart. Consider speaking to students at your local university. If there's an event coming up where a lot of students will be gathered and you have something applicable you can share with them, submit an informal proposal or suggest that you speak. If there aren't any big events like this, that's okay too. You can contact the school's most appropriate department and see if you can talk a professor into inviting you to speak to his or her class. These little tiny opportunities can be really useful for two reasons:

1. They get you more comfortable speaking, which will only serve to make you a better speaker.
2. They can be massaged to look far more impressive than they really are. Speaking anywhere to anyone essentially can be worked into your speaking resume, which will only help you in the long run. It's all about perception and it's all about positioning yourself as an expert in your field.

While it's not always the most experienced speaker who lands the gig – although this is sometimes the case – there is something to be said for the fear of missing out. If someone on the selection committee sees that you've been snatched up by several universities and organizations to speak on your chosen topic, they're going to wonder why those schools thought you were worth their time. They might even get a little competitive and start feeling like they need to have your presence at their event. This doesn't always work, but sometimes showing people through your speaking resume that you do have something worth sharing – and that other people have already validated that – can be the trick you needed.

FINDING SPEAKING OPPORTUNITIES

So, how do you find events? Well, some ways to do that are similar to how you can find awards. For instance, if there's a competitor that you're especially competitive with, you can check out if their leaders have been speaking anywhere. But, you don't want to simply replicate whatever your competitors are doing. You should also do some homegrown research all by yourself. Use search terms like your industry and "event" or your industry and "conference." Also use keywords about your area like "Phoenix" or "Arizona." You should start being able to pull together a list of all potentially relevant events. You can also include one of the following: "call for speakers," "call for proposals," or "call for papers." All of these terms are usually interchangeable and they refer to the window of time during which the event accepts speaking proposals. It's also the section of the website where you should find the requirements for submission and any other information you need to know.

I recommend putting this into something like a Google doc, simply because you can easily make changes and share it with other people. This should be a living document. By that, I mean that you should be going in regularly to see if deadlines for speaking proposals have opened up (or passed you by), if locations and dates have been announced, or if there's anything else that you should know. Here is everything I would include in a grid of speaking opportunities:

- Event Name
- Location
- Dates
- Speaking Proposal Deadline
- URL

You can regularly check this and see at a glance what you're working with.

Once you have your list, it's time to see which ones are actually open for submissions at the current time. Many will not be. Don't be discouraged. You might have found a perfect event where you would absolutely love to speak, but maybe the deadline has already passed.

Oh, and one note about deadlines while we're on the subject is that occasionally you can get an extension. It never hurts to ask, as long as you do so tactfully. If you see that you've just barely missed a deadline you can always write a note like this:

Dear Cindy,

Today, I just stumbled across your conference and am so excited about it. I can't believe I'm just now discovering it! I was really hoping to be able to submit a speaking proposal, but I noticed that the deadline was a few weeks ago. Is there any chance that you would accept a late submission? Or keep one on file in case one of your speakers has to cancel?

Any guidance you can give me is appreciated.

Sincerely,
Rebecca

You might get a big resounding "No" to a note like this, but you also might get a "Yes." I've secured numerous speaking opportunities for people by submitting after a deadline has come and gone. It's not unusual and sometimes it could even work in your favor if they aren't pleased with the quality of the submissions they received thus far. Don't take this as a cue to be late on purpose just to stand out. But, it is worth trying to get an extension if you can
If an extension is impossible, that's okay. Just make sure you ask approximately when the next call for speakers will open and keep that on your radar. These dates often change, so you want to keep checking the website frequently. And if you're bummed about the fact that you've missed a deadline, don't stress. If there's one thing I've learned in my time on this earth, it's that time goes by *so* quickly. Before you know it, next year's call for speakers will be open and you will be able to submit then. With even more experience under your belt, I should add.

For some people, coming up with the proposed topic is a breeze, but for others this poses quite a challenge. If you fall into the latter group, chin up! You're not alone. Many people know that they want to speak and that they have valuable things to say, but still have no idea how to put that all together into a nice pretty package and get someone to accept you.

One tip is to check out past conference agendas and see what other speakers have spoken about. Don't mimic these because you won't be accepted, but you can use these presentation topics to guide you in offering what the event wants in a session. Or try Googling a general topic you're interested in and seeing what recent articles have been written in industry publications. This will inform you about what's trending in the field. A final idea is to offer to speak about a compelling case study (but make sure your customer approves you doing so). Then, just like you would with an article title, piece together a session title that is both informative and intriguing.

Sometimes, when you find a conference, there will be very particular criteria for who can apply to be speakers. Oftentimes this is done so that the amount of self-promotion contained within speaking sessions is limited. This is probably a good idea or else every presentation would probably be a commercial for someone's business, but it can be frustrating if you come up against a roadblock to entry. The most common manifestation of this that I've seen comes when an event does not allow service providers or solution providers to speak. Instead, they demand that end-users or customers share their stories. In this case, you aren't without options. Here are two:

1. One loophole to this is that some conferences allow joint presentations. In this scenario, you and your customer can both offer to speak about your work together and your value proposition will still be conveyed.
2. If they don't allow a joint presentation, then you may still want to consider submitting a willing customer who has a very strong use case with your services or products. Then the customer can act as a mouthpiece on your behalf. Even though you won't get to have the fun of speaking, this can come across as far less subjective to an audience than if you were to present about your company and can be beneficial for your brand.

WRITING A WINNING ABSTRACT

To prepare a solid entry, you want to think of this as a fusion of the techniques I've recommended when approaching contributed articles and awards. For instance, you want to have a very snappy, attention-getting topic title and a data-rich, gripping story with as much hard info as you can. Wishy-washy numbers and lackluster generalities do not fly in the speaking world. This doesn't mean that every single presentation has to be an actual use case, but those are often very well received. If you don't have something like that to offer, you can definitely consider something that is just more along the lines of a "how-to" with actionable advice that would appeal to the attendees. Or you could present something along the lines of industry trends along with your commentary about them. These still should include data and current research to back them up because that is what will set you apart from the other people submitting groundless, opinion-based topics.

The actual submission will usually ask you for information about the proposed speaker (including a bio and headshot), along with an abstract. An abstract is basically an overview of what the speaker is offering to present. I recommend using a talented, competent writer for your abstract because it's what will either get you the gig or get you passed by. The abstract can usually be fairly short, but should explain who the speaker is, what the topic entails and what attendees will gain from it.

Here's a hypothetical example:

Between 2014 and 2015, there has been a 25 percent increase in the number of workout apps purchased. Our society has reached a point in which going to the gym isn't a fitness fanatic's first choice anymore, as advanced technology has conditioned us to crave freedom to do anything (like work out) wherever and whenever we want to. Gyms are losing customers and revenue. In fact, the gym industry lost $30M in profits over the last year alone.

In this session, Daniel Olsen will share the secrets gym owners need to know in order to attract new members to their gyms and retain them for years to come. As the CEO of Gym For Your Life, Olsen will draw from his own personal experiences and patented system for outsmarting the trends that spell doom for gyms.

Attendees will learn:

- *The fatal relationship mistake they've made with their gym members that's hurting their retention rates*
- *How to use the technology that is causing people to leave standard gyms to actually get them in the door*
- *The three things they must do today to prevent member turnover*

The data I inserted there is fake, but be sure you only use recent, founded numbers in your real proposals. Speaking committees like to review information, so presenting something faulty is a surefire way to kill your chances right off the bat.

You can follow this same formula for your proposal, as it's been used countless times for great results. Just be sure to personalize it, include data where you can and make it compelling.

Part X: **Engaging with a PR Agency: Passing the Baton for Success**

So, now you've done the hard work of bootstrapping your own PR efforts, growing your business, gaining some publicity and establishing your brand. Slow clap for you! But, seriously, I'm proud of you. Now it's time to find an agency. You might think you're done once you've signed a commitment on the dotted line, but the work doesn't stop there. Even if you have the best agency you can imagine, there are still things that are going to be required on your part to make your PR efforts a success.

A lot of people unfortunately think that hiring an agency means that they will no longer need to have any involvement in PR and content. But, this is just plain wrong. Before I leave you be to get on with your lovely life, I'm going to walk you through what it takes to find an agency and to engage in a successful and mutually beneficial relationship with the agency once you do.

FINDING AND NARROWING DOWN YOUR OPTIONS

I recommend searching for agencies by asking around. If you know other people in the start-up world, ask them who they're using. They might be working with a PR consultant, and that person could be a great way for you to ease into using someone else's services for PR before having to commit to a larger agency. Or they might have an agency they recommend. You may also get some valuable insight about which agencies to avoid, which is just as important to know. I've grown my business (and have actually had to turn away business due to being too busy) purely by referrals. If a PR consultant or agency is good, other companies should be eager to refer them to you.

If you don't have anybody to ask for recommendations, then it's time to go online. Start with a specific search that includes your industry, business size and "public relations." While huge agencies that cater to a wide variety of clients can still be effective, I highly suggest you start with a specialized team. The agency I was with for several years dealt almost exclusively with funded, high-growth, B2B tech companies. This allowed us to cultivate relationships with the members of the press in this space, become (excruciatingly) familiar with related events and awards and get really good at producing results for our clients. You'll experience similar benefits if you find an agency that proudly proclaims that its mission is centered on businesses like your own.

Once you find a few solid options, ask to review any case studies they have. These should give you a decent idea of how well they've produced for clients in the past. Then, schedule initial meetings with your top three contenders. Explain what you're looking for and see what each comes back with as a proposal. At this point, you should be able to make your decision based on what suggested approach resonates with you the most, what group of people you clicked with best and what your intuition tells you. Then it's time to get a little deeper with your number one choice.

ASKING THE RIGHT QUESTIONS

Before you sign anything, you need to gather a little more information. Here are a few questions to ask to learn more about your chosen agency:

1) On average, how many months (or years) do you work with clients? (This will help you see whether clients are satisfied, as those who remain with the same agency for more than a year typically are pleased with the work.)

2) How do you approach PR strategy? (They should have a clear answer for this that makes sense to you. If they hem and haw, that's a really bad sign).

3) What technology tools do you use to manage and measure your PR work? (This will help you see if they are progressive in the field and are using technology to hold themselves accountable). If they do use technology, ask them how they use it and why. (This will give you further insight into their processes).

4) Who on your team will I be working with most regularly? (You will likely be assigned a junior team member for account management, but should get the verbal commitment that senior executives will still be involved regularly, especially in strategy.)

5) How do you measure success? (If they equate success with helping clients achieve their goals, that's great. Success should be approached strategically and concretely, and with your goals in mind – not theirs). **One extra note here,

courtesy of my former boss. She mentioned that an old metric has resurfaced recently that some agencies are using, which is a poor measurement of success. It's called the Ad Value Equivalency (A.V.E.) and basically means that if an agency gets you a placement in a publication that's the size of an ad, they look at what they would've spent on that if it actually were an ad and multiply it by three (since three times the amount of people typically read an editorial piece over an advertising), and then call that the value of the article. This measurement is ineffective and the mention of using it should be a red flag that makes you run!**

If all their answers are up to snuff, congrats! You have yourself your very own agency.

ESTABLISHING AN ENGAGEMENT

Did you think we were done? Sorry, Charlie. There's still a lot more that goes into effective PR agency engagements. Let's start by talking about expectations. If you're worried about being bothered too much by your PR folks, or even if you aren't, it's best to be very clear about the chain of command and your communication preferences when you first begin working together. You may want to outline clearly who should be responsible for what. For instance, maybe your VP of operations handles all business related materials, but your PR team's daily point of contact is your marketing director. If that's the case, make it clear that you only get pulled in when needed for an interview with press, final approval on your bylines or sensitive company copy. Clarity upfront will save you a lot of headaches later.

Next, let's talk money! While billing might not be the most exciting aspect of working with a PR agency, it's an important one to be particular about as billing related issues often take on lives of their own. First of all, you need to find out how your agency charges you. Some will do it based on hours worked, some will do it with a retainer or some will do it on a project basis. My favorite type of billing is a retainer.

Some people prefer for their agencies to work on an hourly basis because they think it will keep the PR team on track and accountable to a set number of hours. In theory, that sounds like a wise way to do things. However, when an agency tracks time, it also spends a lot of time tracking its time. Every single initiative that a PR person works on for you will have a few extra minutes tacked on just to record the time spent on it. Also, even if you want to see exactly what the hours that you're paying for are being spent on, this doesn't paint the whole picture and can cause you to be in a micromanaging situation. Hopefully after reading this book, you'll understand that there is a lot that goes into PR that is behind the scenes. If you don't understand PR, a lot of things that PR agencies do might seem extraneous and not beneficial to your goals. Of course, you want to hold your agency accountable but I suggest holding them accountable to *results* – not to what's going on behind the scenes because you never know what larger strategy they're working toward.

Here's an example. Hourly billing gets very messy because the agency also, in an effort to make sure it gets its fair pay, will add things in like meetings or travel time spent getting to a meeting with you and your company. That is fair, but it sometimes will cause a little resentment from the company side. If you do a retainer, a lot of these issues will naturally resolve themselves. Your agency will work toward goals and not have to track its hours, and you will have a fixed amount to pay per month. If you are going to go the retainer route, though, the only way this works is if you set very clear goals and frequently measure against how the agency is performing. Be sure to give a little leeway even if all benchmarks aren't hit because of the natural ebbs and flows of the industry though.

The third type of payment form and structure is a project-based engagement. These are also a good idea, but my belief is that PR is always best when worked upon over a steady, long time with larger strategies and goals. So, projects can work – and work well – if you really do have an immediate need. Here are some examples... You have an upcoming event and really want to drive attendance. That'd be okay for a project, but even better for a retainer because the work wouldn't stop when the event does and you could use the momentum for further PR efforts.

People are often worried about not getting enough bang for their buck with a retainer, but you can sometimes actually get *more* this way. I have found in my experience that I end up spending way more hours working on clients I'm on a retainer with than I do working on clients that I'm billing hourly. This is simply because you have goals you're working against so you'll do whatever it takes to reach those goals, whereas hourly based pay doesn't drive you as hard toward goals but rather toward accruing hours.

A final note about billing is to try to have a different point of contact for payment than the people who regularly interact with one another. For instance, when your PR agency sends an invoice to someone, it's best if you have someone in an accounts payable department or removed from PR initiatives to handle that. Collections and money trouble can be extremely divisive, so try to keep it between financial folks and not the ones who are working together daily toward common goals. It's always best if you can remove any chance of something becoming acrimonious before it can ever get there. If it's not possible for you to have degrees of separation between these things, that's okay – just make sure you're very clear in your payment terms and communicate if you're ever going to be late. Just as your agency should over-communicate with you, you should also over-communicate with them.

TIPS FOR A MUTUALLY BENEFICIAL RELATIONSHIP

As with any functioning relationship, both involved parties are responsible for committing to the partnership. Here, I'll outline the things you're liable for, as well as how to keep your agency accountable.

Keeping yourself on track

The number one thing you need to be able and willing to commit to a PR agency when you sign on for its services is... your time. Yes, I know this is the one thing that nobody can make more of and nobody can get back. Time is the most valuable commodity than any of us have and it's also the first thing but none of us wants to give up if we don't have to. If you're the founder of your company or another leader, you may think you can delegate all PR responsibilities to junior members of your staff or even your peers. But, don't be so hasty to do this. It's always best if the top dogs still have a dog in the fight when it comes to PR. Your public image largely defines your company and you want to always make sure you have a hand in shaping it.

This isn't to say you can't delegate any parts of PR to other team members. You definitely can! But, you will still want to have final say in things like the content of press releases when they announce something important, review of articles that are being published with your byline and time spent preparing for – and in conversation with – journalists. This will ensure that your message stays on point and that you retain an active role in your company's success. It will also help position you as a leader who is still in the trenches, which everybody loves.

Something that is okay to delegate to other internal members of your team is the management of your blog, which your PR agency should be handling mostly on its own anyway. But, you can designate somebody to give final approval to blog topics, supply the material for the blog posts or review the written work your agency sends over. You can also have other people on your team review their own bylines and you can elect someone else to be the point person for weekly or more regular PR status updates. But, you should actually be in a meeting with your PR team at least once a month, since this will keep you abreast of what is going on and help you to increase efforts that are working, give feedback, or cut short efforts that just aren't panning out. There is something very powerful about having the founder and senior leadership in control and engaging in PR.

In addition to your time, you're going to need to be responsive to your agency. This is not the same as time. In almost every PR/client relationship I've seen, there's somebody who is a bottleneck. Occasionally it's the PR team itself, but more often than not it's on the client side. It's not usually rooted in malice or a lack of caring; it just happens. But, you will never have a good or effective relationship if you can't be timely.

While many initiatives have long lead times (like speaking opportunities and awards), many others have a tight turnaround. If a PR person gets a reporter on the line, you may need to rearrange your schedule to take the interview when it's convenient for the reporter.

You will also need to let your PR person know immediately what your availability is.

And while things like awards or speaking opportunities should be decided upon as far in advance as possible so no one is scrambling to get things done, sometimes even the most thorough agency will miss seeing an award that is worth pursuing ahead of time. If something like this happens, they might just be able to give you a day or two of notice. Instead of getting mad at them for not being omniscient, be cooperative. Get them the material they need and give them some freedom to make submissions using messaging that's already been approved to save everybody some time.

Also realize that, while most agencies have extensive grids of all the speaking and award opportunities that may be eligible for clients, opportunities can still slip by their notice. This is because a lot of organizations change their deadlines, and new opportunities can pop about of the blue with little to no warning. So, despite an agency's best intentions, there's almost always going to be a bit of that hurry-up-and-scramble, panicky correspondence to push something through on time. As I've mentioned before, your team can always ask for an extension, but this doesn't always guarantee you will get one. So, it's best to try to work within the outlined timeframe as much as you can.

I've seen it happen time and again that leaders within companies get mad at their PR people for what is really the nature of the industry. PR is often frantic, hectic and deadline driven. The simple reason for this is that the news outlets and other organizations that we are at the mercy of are often panicked, pressured and deadline driven. So, we the PR people get the pressure from the journalist and the award organizers, etc. and then we put the heat on you to get us what we need to keep things moving. It's simply how the cookie crumbles, and the sooner you're willing to work with the PR machine, the better the outcome will be for you.

If you're not quick, you could miss out on things. I've heard CEOs and other senior members of leadership say that they are not beholden to their PR agency or they are huffing about why a PR person called him on his cell phone about a copy change on a speaking submission. Let me help you understand this. If something gets submitted to an organization and you're not allowed to edit it later, you're going to be stuck with whatever your PR person happened to write down. So, again, it's best that you have final say. Getting annoyingly repeated affirmation of public-facing material is usually your PR person simply trying to make sure you've approved everything and cover themselves from liability – and your wrath – if the wrong thing is submitted.

One more note is about meetings. Sometimes in meetings, something is proposed that not everybody likes. Generally, I would advise that you defer to the advice of your PR team since they have been doing this a long time and probably have much more hands-on experience than you do, but ultimately it is your business. If something makes you completely uncomfortable, gives you a sinking feeling or causes you to see a bunch of red flags, then you can put the kibosh on it. That's within your power, so don't ever let an agency steamroll you.

Some of what I've told you about is probably leaving you with the feeling that you are beholden to journalists and beholden to your PR agency. This isn't the case, I assure you! I simply am telling you tips that will help you work better with these groups of people because of my own experience. Anytime in business, it's good to be on time, be prompt and go above and beyond for whomever you're dealing with. I'm simply making sure you remember this in particular when it comes to the press and your PR agency. If you follow my advice you will have much better results, I assure you. And the flip side is that these two groups also need to be just as courteous to you, especially your PR team! You are their customer, and they should bend over backward for you, which leads me to the next section...

Holding your agency accountable

If you have specific expectations for your PR agency, be clear about them from the get-go. In your initial conversations, any good company should ask you what your goals are with PR. If they're more concerned with their own goals, or force-fitting a one-size-fits-all program onto your company, run now. If they do ask for your goals, be as specific as possible. If you say something like, "I want awesome brand awareness," you're leaving a heck of a lot of margin in how they can gauge their results. Spend some time thinking about what your real, measurable goals are. Solid PR goals can include things like:

- A specific number of media wins (and specify that this means intentional mentions/profile pieces or contributed articles, not pickups of your press releases)
- A specific number of people who register for and attend your event
- Winning a specific number of awards (or spell out the particular award(s) you want to win)
- Getting a specific percentage increase in traffic to your website
- Landing a specific number of beta customers
- Securing a specific number of media interviews at a tradeshow

Do you see the theme in the goals above? They all include the word "specific." Sure, you may have no concept as to what a realistic number is for any of these goals. But, you can guess. Aim high, and let your PR agency explain whether these benchmarks are feasible. By being unquestionably clear in your goals, you leave no doubt about what is expected and you give your PR team actionable objectives to work toward.

You don't have to feel pressure to have several goals like the ones listed above. If you have just one solid goal, that's fine – great, even! If you have more than one, that's super too. If you have far more goals than can be reasonably pursued, a good PR agency will tell you that and help you narrow down to the ones that are most worth their initial focus. The only mistake you can make with goals is to not have any. If you truly don't have something you're shooting toward, then you need far more help than PR can give you. Have goals and clearly communicate them.

Once you've agreed upon your goals, ask your agency to explain their reporting method to you. There isn't one right or wrong way, but there may be a system that works best for you. Some agencies like to set goals per quarter and then review their progress at the end of each month. Others will set large annual goals, with smaller goals they plan to hit each quarter. Others still may want to work more fluidly and set new objectives at the start of each month that they report on at month's end.

Any of these options can potentially work, although I prefer the first choice. Quarterly goals help you to work toward a larger vision, with monthly status updates that clue you in to whether you're on track or not. It also allows you to be nimble and switch up your goals every quarter if you find some holes in your approach. This is just my opinion. The main idea for you is to find out how your agency proposes you set goals, how they measure against them and how they'll report this information to you. If you are uncomfortable with any of it, say so right away and ask them to compromise with you.

Another logistical element to work out with your team is how they conduct meetings. The approach I recommend is one monthly in-person meeting (unless your agency is in another state), with bi-weekly status calls or emails. A month gives you enough time to see results from the prior meeting, and the more regular status calls helps you get answers you need sooner (or give information the agency needs sooner). I've worked with clients who asked for weekly meetings before, and this can pan out if you or the agency really wants it to. But, my feeling is that meeting weekly uses up too much valuable time on both sides and doesn't give your team enough time to get results in between. However your agency recommends handling meetings, just make sure you agree with the approach and lay out clear expectations.

So, what do you do if you end up in a situation where an agency isn't delivering what you were hoping they would and consistently fails to meet your goals? If you think you might be overly ambitious in the objectives you set, you might want to reevaluate what you're expecting of them. But, if your goals are reasonable, then it's time for an honest conversation. Meet with one of the agency's top leaders and your account representative. Ask them why goals haven't been met and if they think changes can be made to help meet them from here on out. If they're apologetic, amenable and offer solutions, consider giving them another two or three months to see if you end up any happier with what they produce. But, if the team gets defensive, makes excuses or is downright rude, it's time for you to move on.

There are plenty of agencies who would welcome your business with open arms and make sure to treat you right. Let your current team know you will no longer need their services and give them 30 days or so to wrap up any current initiatives (during which time they will need to send you digital copies of everything they've written on your behalf, like articles, award submissions, speaking submissions, etc.). Most PR agencies won't give you the pitches they've written or the media lists they've spent time cultivating, and this is normal. These items are essentially their IP, and much of the information they gather for media lists comes directly from media databases that cost them thousands of dollars per year to subscribe to. Don't be offended or fight them on this. Just accept the other written materials, and move on to brighter and better.

And, this leads me to one last point about keeping your agency accountable... contracts. Even though it's the last thing I'm mentioning, it's something that's super important for you to pay attention to in the beginning. Even though all will seem rosy with your agency in the early stages of the romance, double check any contract they send you for their cancellation clause. Be sure they allow you to cancel with 30-days' notice – or less. Don't even sign a contract that locks you in unfairly or gives you no recourse to end the engagement if you're less than pleased. Also work into the contract that you want copies of all written materials produced for your company at the end of your time working together. If you can swing it, I'd recommend having a lawyer give the contract a quick look-see to make sure there are no other red flags that might be obscured by legal speak. Always best to keep yourself covered!

Part XV: **Arrivederci, My DIY PR Graduates**

So, now we find ourselves coming to the end of our time together – for now, at least. I have to admit I'm kind of sad to see you go. I genuinely hope I've shed some light on the mysterious world of public relations and content, given you actionable advice for taking the reins on your own initiatives and maybe even entertained and enlightened you along the way. I would love to hear about your progress, or field any quick questions I can answer via email. Let me know what you thought of the book (please be gentle! I put my heart into this), and if there's anything I could do to make it better.

You can connect with me at my website, www.diy-publicrelations.com or email me at rebecca@diy-publicrelations.com. And if you're interested in a little extra guidance and hand-holding, the digital kit I've referenced throughout this book is available for purchase on my website. Also, feel free to subscribe to my blog, as I plan to keep my streaming consciousness, references and ideas flowing for you on there.

Most of all, I commend you in your pursuit of creation and freedom. After all, what is entrepreneurship, if not those two things? I know the struggle is real to make your business work, and that some days feel completely overwhelming. But, you just hang in there, trust the process and believe in your abilities. If you live a life you're proud of, and focus on loving those around you, you will win – in business and life.

I'll leave you now with misty eyes (I assure you I'm not kidding – being a mom has made me extra sentimental), and one of my very favorite quotes hopefully to inspire you as it does me:

"To laugh often and much; To win the respect of intelligent people and the affection of children; To earn the appreciation of honest critics and endure the betrayal of false friends; To appreciate beauty, to find the best in others; To leave the world a bit better, whether by a healthy child, a garden patch, or a redeemed social condition; To know even one life has breathed easier because you have lived. **This is to have succeeded.**" -Ralph Waldo Emerson

I wish you endless success, in the most meaningful senses of the word. I can't wait to hear all about it. Cheers to you, your business and your dreams!

Your friend and fan, Rebecca

Special Thanks

This book would not have been possible had it not been for the support, insight and help from some very special people...

HUGE THANKS go to:

You, the entrepreneur. Your spark and tireless pursuit to create new possibilities motivates me to no end!

My PR colleagues, in particular....

- Sarah "Beans" Hawley for being the first person to take a chance on me in the big world of public relations, and always being there to help me. Your savvy tips and generous sharing of knowledge contributed to my career growth more than you know and I value you so much as a friend.
- Aly Saxe for hiring me as your first intern long before I had proven myself, and for taking me under your wing and training me to be a sharp PR pro. Your caring for me over the years and guidance has been so meaningful to me. Also, can't thank you enough for your insights into the technology aspects of PR for this book!
- Kristin Hege for guiding me and showing me the ropes from my very beginning as a PR intern. Your PR skills and successes are undeniable, and you've always been a great friend and person I lean on for advice.
- Jennifer Jewett for helping me to think about PR in new ways! You were influential in shaping my career, and I will always appreciate the time period in which we worked together. You nurtured me professionally and personally, and it meant so much.
- Malcolm Atherton for your significant contributions to this book and your willingness to help my readers understand newswires! It was a pleasure working with you way back when, and again recently!
- Anna Swenson, Valerie Fenyn, Sarah Broome and Matt Simpson for being awesome coworkers and top talent who helped me improve as a PR pro and who I was always proud to work alongside.

- All the clients I worked with during my time at Ubiquity PR. You made me better!
- And last, but certainly not least, I salute all the incredible clients I continue to work with in my own company, Quotable PR & Content. I enjoy every one of you so much and love being able to serve you!

My book team, in particular…
- Laurel Bartlett for being so easy to work with, and masterfully editing my words to ensure the final product is error-free and first class! I appreciate you so very much.
- Clint McFarlin (and Fiero Agency) for your utter design brilliance! I was so stoked to have you design my book cover, and am so proud of the finished product. Your talent is endless.
- Martin Carignan for your design work on the pieces in my digital kit! Even though they're a corollary to this book, it's important to me that they reflect the book's messages and are helpful to the entrepreneurs who use them. You did truly wonderful work, and I'm so pleased!

My friends, in particular…
- Canyon, for being my BF4L for over two decades and being like a sister to me. I cannot imagine life without you and am lucky to have your beautiful soul as a constant presence in my life (and in Demi's)! Your support and friendship is invaluable.

My family, in particular…
- Nini and Erin, for your support of – and excitement about – this endeavor. Your enthusiasm helped me to make it to the finish line! You both mean so much to me.
- My dad. You raised me with roots and wings, and the confidence to know I can do literally anything I set my mind to. I count having you as my daddy as one of my very greatest blessings!
- My mom, for too many things to count. Thank you for helping me with all the late nights and hard work this book required. You are always there in the seemingly small moments that others don't see, but that make all the difference. You've

taught me to pursue my dreams and given me every opportunity to do so. Demi and I are beyond blessed to have you as such a central part of our lives!

- Todd, for your unwavering belief in me and for being the best sounding board I could ask for. Thank you for your special place in my life and for always taking care of your girls and treating us like gold. You are irreplaceable.

- Ollie, for being the best big brother that Demi could have! Your daddy and I are so proud of you, and your sister thinks you hung the moon itself! Your part in our lives inspires me greatly.

- My Demi, for your smile that powers me through hard work and any obstacles I encounter! I hope to make you very proud. I consider it the greatest privilege that I get to be your mommy. Thank you for being the most rewarding gift I've ever been given.

www.ingramcontent.com/pod-product-compliance
Lightning Source LLC
Chambersburg PA
CBHW051320170526
45166CB00002B/618